Pastoral Care and the Parish

Faith and the Future
General Editor: David Nicholls

Choices
Ethics and the Christian
David Brown

Church and Nation
Peter Cornwell

Pastoral Care and the Parish
Peter Davie

The Faith Abroad
John D. Davies

Church, Ministry and Unity
A Divine Commission
James E. Griffiss

The Authority of Divine Love
Richard Harries

The Bible
Fountain and Well of Truth
John Muddiman

Faith, Prayer and Devotion
Ralph Townsend

Sacraments and Liturgy
The Outward Signs
Louis Weil

Pastoral Care and the Parish

Peter Davie

Basil Blackwell

First published 1983
Basil Blackwell Publisher Limited
108 Cowley Road, Oxford OX4 1JF, England

British Library Cataloguing in Publication Data
Davie, Peter
    Pastoral care and the parish. — (Faith and
    the future)
    1. Church of England—Clergy
    2. Pastoral theology
    I. Title   II. Series
    253   BV4011

    ISBN 0-631-13225-2
    ISBN 0-631-13226-0 Pbk

Typesetting by Cambrian Typesetters, Aldershot, Hants
Printed in Great Britain by T.J. Press Ltd, Padstow

Contents

In memory of my father
Sidney Samuel Pearce Davie
born 23 December 1904
died 16 October 1982

Foreword

This book is one of a series whose writers consider some important aspects of Christianity in the contemporary scene and in so doing draw inspiration from the Catholic revival in the Anglican Communion which began in Oxford one hundred and fifty years ago. This revival — with its thinkers, pastors, prophets, social reformers and not a few who have been held to be saints — has experienced changes in the understanding of the Christian faith since the time of the Tractarians and has none the less borne witness to themes which are deep and unchanging. Among these are the call to holiness, the communion of saints, the priesthood of the Church and its ministers and a sacramental religion, both otherworldly and with revolutionary claims upon man's social life.

I am myself convinced that the renewal of the Church for today and tomorrow needs a deep recovery of these themes of Catholic tradition and a vision of their contemporary application. The books of this series are designed towards this end, and I am sure that readers will be grateful for the help they give. Many are thirsty but 'the well is deep'.

+ Michael Ramsey

Preface

The renewal of pastoral care and parish life of the Church of England was one of the chief concerns of the leaders of the Oxford Movement. Newman's first Tract for the Times was a passionate appeal to the clergy to recognize that they had been commissioned by Christ and anointed by the Holy Spirit in ordination. Theirs was not a merely secular avocation, but a sacred ministry dedicated to the service of the Church of God.

Clergy and ordinands who came under the spell of this teaching began to approach the pastoral ministry with a new sense of devotion and purpose. The Oxford Movement, along with the Evangelical Revival, led to a great renewal in the parishes of the Victorian Church of England.

My aim in this book is to sketch some of the main features of this pastoral revival in mid-Victorian Anglo-Catholic parishes, and then to consider what we can learn from it today. In thinking about the present and future I extend my view to take in recent developments in the Christian Church as a whole, especially those associated with the teachings and influence of the Second Vatican Council.

Several chapters are prefaced by quotations from the Canon Law of the Church of England. I have included these excerpts from the Church's laws because they show clearly what the Church expects in the sphere of pastoral ministry — what we have to live up to.

Many topics are inevitably missed in a short book on a large subject. One that should be mentioned is that of prayer. Rightly regarded as fundamental to pastoral care, it needs a whole book to itself, and I refer the interested reader to the relevant volume in this series.

I wish to thank my friends David Nicholls and Perry Butler for their many helpful suggestions on improvements to the original manuscript. They are not responsible, of course, for the result. Above all gratitude is due to my wife, Elisabeth, both for typing the manuscript and for her ever cheerful encouragement.

Peter Davie
Canterbury

1 The Anglican Tradition of Pastoral Care

From Canon C24 Of Priests Having a Cure of Souls

1. Every priest having a cure of souls shall provide that, in the absence of reasonable hindrance, Morning and Evening Prayer daily and on appointed days the Litany shall be said in the church, or one of the churches, of which he is the minister.

2. Every priest having a cure of souls shall, except for some reasonable cause approved by the bishop of the diocese, celebrate, or cause to be celebrated, the Holy Communion on all Sundays and other great Feast Days and on Ash Wednesday, and shall diligently administer the sacraments and other rites of the Church.

3. Every priest having a cure of souls shall, except for some reasonable cause approved by the bishop of the diocese, preach or cause to be preached, a sermon in his church at least once each Sunday.

4. He shall instruct the children, or cause them to be instructed, in the Christian faith; and shall use such opportunities of teaching or visiting in the schools within his cure as are open to him.

5. He shall carefully prepare, or cause to be prepared, all such as desire to be confirmed and, if satisfied of their fitness, shall present them to the bishop for confirmation.

6. He shall be diligent in visiting his parishioners, particularly those who are sick and infirm; and he shall provide opportunities whereby any of his

parishioners may resort unto him for spiritual counsel and advice.

The Canons of the Church of England, second edition,
Church Information Office, 1975

GEORGE HERBERT'S COUNTRY PARSON

The classical description of the traditional Anglican ideal of the cure of souls (or pastoral care) is that sketched in George Herbert's *Country Parson*. Drawing upon a few years of intense experience as parish priest of the village of Bemerton near Salisbury, Herbert wrote his famous and influential book a short while before his early death in 1633. Two centuries later it inspired John Keble, the elder statesman of the Oxford Movement, in his life's work as parish priest of the Hampshire village of Hursley.

According to Herbert a priest was 'the deputy of Christ for the reducing of men to the obedience of God'. In contrast to the Protestant emphasis upon the individual's direct relationship with God, Herbert stressed the role of the visible and sacramental Church.

For Herbert the Catholic tradition of the worship of God in and through corporate liturgical prayer was at the heart of pastoral care and the life of the parish. Each morning and evening the bell of Bemerton church was rung to summon his family and parishioners to Morning Prayer at ten and Evening Prayer at four. The corporate and liturgical forms of worship provided in the Book of Common Prayer were the basic framework of Herbert's life as pastor.

Catholicism is a sacramental religion, so Herbert stressed the importance and proper use of the two 'Gospel sacraments of Baptism and Holy Communion'. The Anglican reformers of the sixteenth century attempted to restore the early church practice of weekly Communion but failed to overcome the conservatism of the laity. They had grown used to attendance at Mass chiefly as a means of witnessing the sacred moment of consecration when bread and wine became the Body and Blood of Christ. The idea of receiving communion regularly had been lost and proved impossible to revive. However Herbert tried to make the best of the situation by suggesting that 'the Parson celebrates it, if not duly once a month, yet at least five or six times in a year: as at Easter, Christmas, Whitsuntide, afore and after Harvest, and at the beginning of Lent.' Each celebration was a great and solemn occasion, impelling the parson to stir up his flock 'with catechizings and lively exhortations on the Sundays before the Communion Sunday.' As to Baptism, it was stressed that the parish priest was to strive assiduously to persuade his flock to have their babies baptized publicly on 'Sundays or great days.'

The Book of Common Prayer provided the basis for the faithful discharge of the pastoral ministry of worship. Together with the Bible it was also the basis of the ministry of the word. The country parson was above all a teacher who preached 'constantly' from the pulpit, for it was 'his joy and throne'. He was to use all his skill to gain attention but he was not to set out to show himself 'witty, or learned, or eloquent, but holy'. For 'the character of his sermons was holiness.' He also valued catechizing highly and taught his flock in church every Sunday afternoon. Basing his course upon the catechism provided in the Book of Common Prayer, he set out to 'infuse a competent knowledge of salvation in every one of his flock', and to instruct them how to put this knowledge into practice in devotion and Christian living. Beyond the set occasions of sermon or catechism, the minister was to use all possible opportunities (such as visiting) for instruction, and indeed his whole life and that of his family should be an object lesson to his parishioners.

Great emphasis was also placed upon the pastoral ministry of service. The pastor was to visit constantly 'upon the afternoons in the weekdays', especially the sick and afflicted. He was to follow 'the Church's counsel' in persuading the sick 'to special confession', to give to charity, and to receive Holy Communion. The priest was a man 'full of charity', open-handed with the poor. As well

3

as his services as a priest, he was to offer 'all to his parish' for he was to serve them as 'not only a pastor but a lawyer also, and a physician'. The knowledge required for these services was not extensive and could be gained from a few textbooks.

The heart of the country parson's life was his constant devotion to prayer and study. Prayer was chiefly offered through the devout performance of the liturgical services of the church. Study was focused on the Bible, for 'the chief and top of his knowledge consists in the book of books, the Holy Scriptures.'

Herbert's ideal, taken up again by Keble and the Oxford Movement in the nineteenth century, was to make the English country parish a colony of heaven. All parishioners were to be drawn into the liturgical worship of the parish church through the devout and tireless ministrations of their priest as their teacher and pastor. His aim in teaching was to lead all to holiness of life. They were never to be satisfied but were to be continually urged to press on to ever greater conformity to the pattern of Christ their Saviour. All the while their pastor tended them like a father, caring for them in poverty, sickness and all the vicissitudes of life. Such was the ideal Herbert bequeathed to subsequent generations of Anglican pastors.

TWO VICTORIAN PRIESTS

When I was the rector of a village parish on the edge of the Cotswolds I became very interested in the life and work of one of my Victorian predecessors. Jacob Clements, the young parson who tolled the bell at his induction in 1846, was one of a new breed of dedicated high church priests who were inspired by the ideals of the Oxford Movement to renew the lives of their parishes along Catholic lines.

The Oxford Movement had begun in 1833 as an attempt to revive the Church of England by recalling her priests to the ideals that had inspired George Herbert and the high church movement of the seventeenth century. By the time John Henry Newman seceded from the Church of England in 1845 the movement had lost impetus in Oxford, but its influence was growing rapidly in the parishes.

At Upton St Leonards Jacob Clements spent fourteen vigorous years translating Anglo-Catholic principles into practice. The Oxford Movement had above all stressed the importance of the sacraments: at Upton as in many other parishes this was reflected in the restoration of the neglected chancel to make it a worthy setting for the celebration of the Eucharist. Anglo-Catholics stressed the importance of teaching the faith: in 1849 with the financial assistance of the local landowner Clements built a fine stone school for the village children, replacing the inadequate dame school on the edge of the churchyard. Clements was also vigorous in promoting coal and clothing clubs and other forms of self-help among the poor. It is evident from the records of these and other activities still to be found in the parish chest that Clements set out to make the church the basis of the social life of the village.

While Clements was building up church life at Upton a more well-known young priest was pursuing similar aims in the Berkshire market town of Wantage. William John Butler was widely regarded as the model Anglo-Catholic priest of the post-Oxford Movement generation. Fortunately he kept a pastoral diary which I will be using in later chapters to help build up a picture of Anglo-Catholic pastoral care.

ANGLO-CATHOLIC PASTORAL CARE

Parish priests like Clements and Butler were concerned to put the principles of the Oxford Movement into practice. The basic principle of Anglo-Catholicism was its sacramentalism. Where Protestants stressed the direct unmediated relationship between man and God, Anglo-Catholics insisted that God communicates with man through nature, through Jesus Christ, and through the

Church, its ministry and its sacraments. The practical consequence of this was that the sacraments provided the basis of the pastoral system.

Evangelicals insisted that the Christian life began with conversion: Baptism merely prefigured this in the case of infants or ratified it in the case of adults. Anglo-Catholics were equally insistent that the new life began in infant Baptism. This high view of the importance of the sacrament led to a change in pastoral practice. Before the Oxford Movement most Baptisms, apart from those of the poor whose houses were too small, took place in private homes. The Anglo-Catholics attempted to re-establish the Prayer Book ideal of public Baptism.

Christian initiation was completed in Confirmation. The Catholic view was that it was a sacrament in which further gifts of the Holy Spirit were communicated to establish, strengthen and perfect the grace of Baptism. The acceptance of this view led to the introduction of special classes and to a more devout ordering of the Confirmation service than had often been the case in the eighteenth century.

The Eucharist was at the heart of the Catholic idea of pastoral care. Prior to the Oxford Movement celebrations were infrequent: usually three, four or five times a year in most parishes. Now the norm became a celebration each Sunday and holy day. The new emphasis upon eucharistic devotion was associated with belief in the real presence of Christ in the sacrament.

Evangelicals and Anglo-Catholics had a common longing for holiness of life, but where Protestants sought holiness solely in a direct personal relationship with God, Anglo-Catholics stressed the value of priestly absolution and spiritual guidance.

Baptism, Confirmation, Eucharist and Confession formed the basis of pastoral care. Through them the parish priest mediated grace to his flock, enabling them to respond to his teaching about the Christian life.

Teaching was of great importance because it was necessary to know and believe revealed truth. The aim was not intellectual training (the current secular view) but a devout understanding of Christian doctrinal and moral teaching. Education was essentially spiritual and so the clergy must be in charge of parochial schools, to symbolize and enforce the supremacy of holiness over cleverness. The Prayer Book catechism was the ideal mode of teaching, because it dealt with Christian doctrine and morals in the context of worship. Not all children attended day school, and it was therefore necessary to supplement it by providing a Sunday school. Children were gathered into church for instruction by voluntary lay teachers, under the direction of the parish priest.

Preaching was mainly for instruction in faith and morals. Parishioners were to be moved to practice sacramental and personal devotion, and to obey the moral law. Preaching was often supplemented by communicant groups, or guilds, aimed at deepening the spiritual life.

As well as administering the sacraments and teaching, the good parish priest also exercised his ministry of pastoral care by visiting his flock. Visitation of the sick and dying had priority because sickness was to lead to repentance. The dying lay poised between heaven and hell. It was the priest's solemn task to soften hard hearts and to minister absolution. The visitation of the healthy was, in a way, more difficult, for lack of a sense of need often made it difficult to steer conversations to spiritual matters.

As mediator between heaven and earth, the priest rooted the social order in eternal values and sanctions. The parish was to be a colony of heaven, a harmonious order in which the social classes were bound together by the mutual rights and duties taught them by the Church.

Anglo-Catholics believed firmly in the parish system as the local unit of civil and church administration. The Church was the Church of all the people.

THE SCOPE OF PASTORAL CARE

At the head of this chapter I have quoted Canon C24, which sets out the duties the Church of England expects its parish priests to perform. These correspond closely with the descriptions given by Herbert in the seventeenth century and Butler in the Victorian age. The priest's basic duties are the recitation of the daily offices and the administration of the Church's rites and sacraments (sections 1 and 2). The rest of his time is chiefly occupied by preaching and teaching (sections 3 to 5) and with the demands of pastoral visitation and counselling (section 6).

In what follows I shall be concerned to describe these traditional duties in more detail, using evidence provided by George Herbert and by William John Butler. At the same time, however, I will be concerned to discuss how the ways in which these duties are performed have changed in relation to changes in society and the Church. The modern parish priest is a teacher like Herbert and Butler before him, but what he teaches and the way he teaches are not the same.

Canon C24 refers to the cure of souls; I use the term more widely accepted today, 'pastoral care', but understand it to refer to all aspects of the parish priest's pastoral work in the same way as indicated by Canon C24. Nowadays the term 'pastoral care' is often used in a restricted sense which equates it with counselling. My use of it is based upon the traditional broader understanding.

FURTHER READING

Peter Hammond, *The Parson and the Victorian Parish*, Hodder and Stoughton, 1977

George Herbert, *The Country Parson*, *The Temple*, SPCK, 1981

Anthony Russell, *The Clerical Profession*, SPCK, 1980

The Country Parson has been published in many editions over the years. The new edition given above has a helpful introduction. Hammond provides a good general survey of the Victorian situation. Russell discusses the parish priest's changing role over recent centuries.

2 Change in Church and Society

THE FAILURE OF THE ANGLICAN IDEAL

In 1850 John Keble wrote a lengthy review of Edward Monro's new book on *Parochial Work*, hailing it as 'our new "Country Parson" '. For Keble Herbert's prescriptions were as relevant as they had been when first written down more than two centuries before. Monro's work was to be prized because it adapted the old tradition virtually unchanged to the needs of the early Victorian country parish. A shorter period of time separates us from Keble and Monro, yet many of their ideas cannot be made relevant to our situation without very considerable adaptation. Keble was a conservative with a somewhat blinkered view of the pastoral situation. He thought solely in terms of the old rural social order, which even as he wrote was being replaced by an industrial society he seemed hardly aware of.

Central to the pastoral ideal of Herbert and of the Oxford Movement was the claim of the Church of England to be the church of all the people. The whole country was divided into dioceses which were subdivided into parishes. The parish church claimed the allegiance of all those who lived within the parochial boundary; the duty of caring for all of them was laid upon the parish priest.

However even in Herbert's time there were those who rejected the Anglican Church, either because they belonged to some other Christian body or because they were indifferent to the claims of Christianity altogether. In the early seventeenth century some of this defection was masked by the legal enforcement of church attendance,

9

but by the mid-nineteenth century it was all too evident that traditional Anglican aspirations were beyond realization.

In 1851 the official census of church attendance taken that year confirmed that while the Church of England might claim that the majority of the population belonged to it through Baptism, its parish churches only attracted about half of those who regularly attended places of worship. The other half were to be found in the chapels of Protestant Dissenters: the Baptists, Methodists and Congregationalists, whose numbers had grown so greatly under the impulse of the Evangelical revival.

THE MISSING WORKING CLASS

The census also confirmed a widespread suspicion that the majority of the industrial working class were non-church-goers. One crucial change accompanying industrialization was the rapid growth of towns and cities. From the end of the eighteenth centry onwards the ever-growing demands of mines and factories for labour drew thousands of new inhabitants into towns and cities from the surrounding rural areas. The census showed that generally there were higher levels of church attendance in the countryside than in the towns, and that in most cases the larger the town the lower the level of church attendance. This was evident particularly in the figures for London and the new industrial cities like Birmingham, Manchester and Leeds.

Detailed examination of the evidence shows that the very lowest levels of church attendance were associated with the poorest central urban areas, with only slightly higher levels in more respectable working-class areas a little further out. More people attended a place of worship in mixed working and middle class areas like Hackney or Handsworth, but it was only in the outer respectable middle class suburbs like Hampstead or Edgbaston that a considerable proportion of the population was found to attend church.

The pattern of low levels of working class church attendance was confirmed by subsequent unofficial censuses. At the end of Queen Victoria's reign a Bishop of Stepney remarked that in the East End of London not one man in a hundred was to be found in church on a Sunday. The same bishop also argued that it was not that the Church had lost the working class, for 'it had never had them'. This opinion is confirmed by recent studies of the problem.

Pre-industrial England was never wholly Christianized. There is evidence of religious indifference and of hostility towards the Church in George Herbert's time and earlier. In the seventeenth century legal penalties were used to enforce compliance. In the subsequent century, although this form of control had fallen into disuse, it was still possible for landowners and farmers to dragoon their labourers into Sunday appearances at the parish church. The parson rewarded their efforts by teaching that it was God who had ordered society into ranks. It was the duty of labourers to accept their low station in life with humility and to fulfil their duties faithfully towards those set above them. Where they could, labourers escaped from the Church of England into indifference, or became Methodist. Either way they achieved a measure of independence.

In the rapidly growing towns and cities no one could enforce church attendance, so on Sundays labourers were free to do as they wished — lie in bed, go to the pub or visit relations. A pattern of life was established which for the great majority did not include churchgoing.

The Church of England was identified as the church of the upper and middle classes. Labourers who did venture into church were often made to sit in the worst seats and felt uncomfortable among their better-dressed 'superiors'. Widespread resentment was aroused by the practice of holding out charitable gifts as baits to lure the poor into church.

Nevertheless no more than a small minority were atheists or secularists. Most working-class children learned the rudiments of Christian faith at Sunday school, and workers appeared in church for the rites of passage. The Church's rites of Baptism, Matrimony and Burial were

11

accepted by the majority of the Victorian working class as the proper ceremonies to mark the important transitions in life of birth, marriage and death.

Much pastoral effort was concentrated upon winning the allegiance of the working class in the Victorian and Edwardian periods, but with little success. By the end of the First World War it was evident that the high hopes of the Victorian pastoral revival were to remain unfulfilled.

THE MIDDLE CLASS GAINED AND LARGELY LOST

In contrast, Victorian middle-class life was greatly influenced by the Evangelical revival and by the Oxford Movement. Churchgoing was the norm. The Bible was read, family prayers were said, and charitable works performed. The Church of England was strongest in middle-class suburbs.

The rot set in during the final third of the nineteenth century. The decade after 1860 was a critical one. The publication of Darwin's *Origin of Species* in 1859 was followed a year later by the equally shocking attack on existing views of the Bible in *Essays and Reviews*. Unbelief and doubt became common among the educated, and questionings percolated down into middle and working class minds.

The habit of worship was also eroded by social changes. Sunday train-trips became popular, and later motor cars added to people's ability to get away from the towns in their free time. The Victorian Sunday was eroded and with it collapsed the automatic association between churchgoing and respectability.

THE CHURCH'S DECLINING ROLE IN SOCIETY

In the pastoral ideal of Herbert and of Keble the Church of England both provided the basic ideas of society and controlled its important activities. The story of the past two centuries is the story of the erosion of that ideal.

Theology is no longer the queen of the sciences. Men do

not look to religion for the solution of their problems. In pre-modern times both the existence and operation of the world were explained in terms of God and supernatural causes. Prayer was seen as a solution when man reached the limits of his powers (as he often did). Today we turn to the physical sciences for explanations of the workings of nature. God no longer figures as an explanation; what happens in nature is to be understood wholly in terms of forces within nature itself. Similarly we turn to the doctor and the resources of scientific medicine when we fall ill. In the twentieth century scientific knowledge has grown so as to dominate all aspects of human life. Keble claimed to speak authoritatively on human nature, education and moral development, on the basis of theological tradition alone. Now we have to take into account the findings and theories of psychologists, psychotherapists and educationalists. The modern pastor cannot remain content with the simple prescriptions of Herbert or his Victorian descendants.

In the nineteenth century Anglo-Catholics fought a losing battle, trying to hold on to their claimed monopoly of the provision of social services (to use a modern term) like education and welfare work with the poor. In the twentieth century the Church's stake in these services has been steadily whittled away. Similarly the Church has largely lost the role it claimed of providing society with its basic morals and ideas. The state and other institutions within society operate largely independently of the Church.

THE CHURCH AND THE CHURCHES

I noted earlier that the 1851 census confirmed the widespread belief that the Church of England and the Dissenters commanded roughly equal numbers of active adherents. Over the past century or so the Protestant Free Churches have declined even more rapidly than the Church of England, and are but pale shadows of their Victorian selves. At the same time the number of Roman Catholics has expanded, so that now they can count on national church attendances roughly equal in number to those of the Anglicans.

Victorian Anglo-Catholic priests dismissed the claims of non-Anglicans. They would settle for nothing less than complete monopoly, so sure were they of the soundness of their case. Now we are not only aware that monopoly is not a practical possiblity; we have also come to accept our fellow Christians as truly members of the Body of Christ.

CHANGES IN PASTORAL THEOLOGY

Much of the inspiration for the more open and positive attitudes of modern Catholics towards their fellow Christians comes from the teachings of the Second Vatican Council which met in Rome from 1962 to 1965. Its teachings are also important to us because they signal an important shift in theological thought. In contrast to the negative and conservative tone of most Roman Catholic teaching over the previous several centuries, Vatican II was evidently animated by a more open and positive attitude towards the modern world.

In his opening speech to the assembled bishops, Pope John XXIII clearly distinguished between the substance of the faith and its particular formulations. He recognized the need for responsible attempts to re-express the Christian faith in terms intelligible to modern men. A revitalized theology was needed to engage in a dialogue with modern thought. The teachings of Vatican II include much that is relevant to the theme of this book. In a number of its documents the council touched on subjects like the relationship between pastoral theology and psychology, changes in the theology of marriage, and the role of the parish priest.

The mid-nineteenth century Anglo-Catholic movement was largely backward-looking and conservative. This was reflected in the views on pastoral care of men like W.J. Butler. It was not until the final decades of the century that leaders like Bishop Gore attempted a *rapprochement* between orthodox Christianity and modern ideas. The

14

influence of this new approach was gradually felt in the parishes of late Victorian and Edwardian England, and was evident in new attitudes to religious education, the treatment of the poor and so on. Many of the ideas of that time now seem old-fashioned, but what is not redundant is the spirit which inspired them.

This book seeks to examine approaches to pastoral care inspired by the Oxford Movement. Although the early Anglo-Catholics tended to be backward-looking and out of touch (and sympathy) with modern society, the essentials of their ideas on pastoral care still have much to teach us. The more recent pastoral ideas of Vatican II and of outstanding Roman Catholic theologians, like Karl Rahner, can guide us in the necessary reinterpretation of the Catholic pastoral tradition along lines similar to those pioneered by those liberal Anglo-Catholics who shared the ideals of Bishop Gore at the beginning of this century.

FURTHER READING

W.M. Abbott (ed), *The Documents of Vatican II*, America Press, NY, 1966

Alan D. Gilbert, *The Making of Post-Christian Britain*, Longman, 1980

David F. Wright (ed), *Essays in Evangelical Social Ethics*, Paternoster Press, 1978

Abbott's book contains the full texts of the documents from Vatican II quoted in this book. Gilbert's work is a recent social history of modern Christianity. Wright's work is chiefly valuable in relation to the subject of this chapter for the essay by John Briggs on 'From Christendom to Pluralism'.

3 The Parish and the Local Church

THE PARISH SYSTEM

The parish has served as the basic form of local church organization for more than a thousand years. Its success was due to its simplicity: one man in charge of pastoral care in a given area. Because it corresponded to the organization of the basic structures of social life, almost everything of importance associated with work and home took place within the confines of the rural parish. Here the priest was in touch with all aspects of life, secular as well as religious. Indeed it was hard to draw the line between the secular and the religious, so closely were they integrated. We have seen how at Bemerton George Herbert was in touch with his parishioners not only on religious occasions, like baptisms, but also in relation to secular activities like the dispensing of medicines or the teaching of reading. The altar of the parish church was the heart of the social order. In villages in which all were known and had their place, the Church invoked a supernatural blessing upon the whole of life.

From the mid-nineteenth century onwards, it became increasingly apparent that the old parish system was beginning to break down. The early supporters of the Oxford Movement shared a widespread contemporary dislike of industrial society and looked back longingly to the parish of the rural past. But the clock could not be turned back, for now the majority of the population lived in large towns. There the parish remained as the basic unit of church organization, but even diligent priests with dedicated staffs could not reproduce the old rural ideal. Despite the frequent subdivision of large town parishes and the creation of mission churches, it proved impossible to be in effective contact with more than a minority of the population. Vestiges of the old ideal remained in that the parish church was widely used for the rites of passage (Baptism, Matrimony and Burial), but, for most people, these contacts with the Church were fleeting episodes in lives otherwise spent outside church influences. Even the elaborate network of Edwardian church organizations for children, 'lads', mothers, working men and the elderly failed to rebuild the old ideal of the local community.

Not only has the modern town parish a population too vast and shifting for the Church to maintain effective contact; there are also problems associated with the fact that for most people their place of work is very often some distance from their homes. Consequently even if the Church can make contact with them it only relates to part of their lives. In recent years various attemps have been made, with varying success, to supplement parochial work with chaplaincies to industry and other places of work.

The parish church in the modern town cannot hope to play the same role as the church in the rural parish, but it can become a living community serving the wider society that surrounds it. The widespread use of the Parish Communion, accompanied by breakfast or coffee, has been a pioneering effort in this respect. This has led in some parishes to the celebration of house-communions and the development of groups for prayer and Bible study. Many now see the future of the Church in a return to something like the pattern of the early Christian groups which met in houses to hear the word of God and celebrate the Eucharist.

THE LOCAL CHURCH

The Church of England is the guardian of a heritage of ancient and beautiful church buildings. They are a responsibility that cannot be wished away and, indeed, fulfil a positive purpose in being visible reminders of the presence of God. In practice this responsibility has to be balanced against the primary need to build up the local church as a living community 'not built with stones'. In a post-Christian society such as ours there are no social props for religious belief and practice. Merely conventional churchgoing is not strong enough to survive in a hostile or indifferent environment. There is an increasing need for groups of committed Christians who will give each other mutual support in learning to pray, to study and to practise the faith. The declining numbers of clergy will be needed more and more for their proper task of guiding and helping these groups. They will not prove to be good stewards of their time if they spend too much of it on secondary fund-raising activities to support church buildings or equipment. It is possible to envisage some future parishes dispensing with church buildings altogether (getting rid of an architecturally worthless building or not building where there is no church), meeting in small groups in houses and coming together occasionally in school halls. Certainly more can be done to extend the practice of sharing the use of one building among churches of different denominations.

It is unrealistic to ignore the fact that for many churchgoers what means most to them is a particular building invested with its memories and associations. This is not in itself wrong: the first Christians of necessity had no buildings and they did eventually build when they were able to do so. A Catholic recognizes that the use of church buildings is a proper extension of the sacramental principle that the material and the particular focus the attention on a universal and spiritual God.

As well as balancing this devotion against the necessities of finance and the proper use of time already discussed, we also have to bear in mind that the local church building can become an end it itself. Too many churchgoers show little interest beyond the confines of St Agatha's or St Bernard's. The local church is not an end in itself: it exists to serve the kingdom of God; it should point beyond itself. Self-centred ('parochial' in the worst sense) attitudes simply contradict the message the Church exists to proclaim. Whatever form local church life takes, it must be shaped by the principles the church lives to serve, if it is to be more than a social club.

THE CHURCH'S ROLE

Having touched on some of the problems of the traditional parish and some suggested reforms, I shall conclude this chapter with an outline of the role of the local church which will provide a starting point for my discussion of the work of pastoral care.

In Vatican II's *Dogmatic Constitution on the Church* there is a brief section (26) which makes it clear that the local church is more than a minor branch of head office: it is the Church in its locality: 'The Church of Christ is truly present in all legitimate local congregations . . . for local churches, united with their pastors, are themselves called churches in the New Testament . . . in their own locality Christians constitute the new people of God.'

The main purpose for which the local church is gathered together is to celebrate the Eucharist in which the mystery of the 'Lord's Supper is celebrated [and] the whole brotherhood joined together.' Although these communities are 'frequently small and poor', nevertheless 'Christ is present in them'. The role of this Christ-filled community is to take part in God's mission in the world through teaching, witness and service. An account of some of these activities will occupy us in subsequent chapters of this book. Before we deal with these topics, however, it is necessary to touch on the subject of preaching, for, according to the Vatican fathers, the church 'is gathered together by the ministry of the word'. In a post-Christian society men will not come into the Church and stay there as a matter of course: they must be effectively convinced by the proclamation of the word of the Gospel.

FURTHER READING

Karl Rahner, *The Shape of the Church to Come*, SPCK, 1974
Michael Winter, *Mission Resumed?*, Darton, Longman and Todd, 1979
These two books discuss the role of the local church today in the light of the need for radical changes.

4 Preaching

PROCLAIMING THE WORD

A Methodist minister described how as a theological student he tried to explain to a puzzled Iranian student what he would do in his future work as a minister. His questioner failed to understand how a young man could presume to counsel others on religious and ethical questions. In his society it was the province of old men to advise others out of the wisdom acquired by experience. The ordinand's answer was that the Christian minister did not speak of the fruits of his own wisdom but proclaimed the revealed Word of God: it was possible for him to speak about the ultimate questions of life because his message rested on a wisdom not his own.

The same emphasis upon the proclamation of the Word of God as the 'distinctive and prime duty' of priests 'as co-workers with their bishops' is evident in the teachings of the Second Vatican Council. Proclamation is made through the priest's life, leadership, celebration of the sacraments, and preaching.

The Church began with the proclamation that Jesus had risen, and those who heard and responded with faith were baptized. They became members of a priestly body whose responsibility it was to proclaim the good news. According to Vatican II Christian priesthood derives from the priesthood of Christ. He is the sole mediator between God and man, but through Baptism his followers share in his priesthood. Their task is to proclaim the good news of reconciliation between God and man through Christ. Within the priestly body, bishops and priests are set apart with a special responsibility to proclaim the Gospel and to bring men into the Church, to share in the Eucharist and to take their part in bringing men to God.

Preaching was singled out by the council as a primary task of this ministerial priesthood, alongside the administration of the sacraments.

> Among the principal duties of the bishop [shared by priests] the preaching of the Gospel occupies an eminent place. For bishops are preachers of the faith who lead new disciples to Christ. They are authentic teachers . . . endowed with the authority of Christ, who preached to the people committed to them the faith they must believe and put into practice (*Dogmatic Constitution on the Church*, section 25).

In the course of Christian history there have been differences between Protestants and Catholics about the place of preaching in pastoral work. At the time of the Reformation Protestants objected to the idea of a priesthood that mediated grace through the sacraments. Their conception of the minister was that of a man who was primarily a preacher. In Protestant churches the altar was replaced by the pulpit as the focus of attention. The minister's work of pastoral visitation was an extension of his pulpit ministry in that he used his entry to people's homes as a further opportunity to proclaim God's word through exhortation and teaching.

In reaction Roman Catholics further emphasized the idea

of the priest as primarily one who celebrates Mass. The importance of preaching was not denied, but priesthood was defined primarily in cultic terms.

In the nineteenth century this Protestant—Catholic difference divided the Church of England. Evangelical clergymen concentrated on preaching to the neglect of the sacraments, and Anglo-Catholics held that although preaching was important as a means of instruction, it was subordinate to the sacraments as the true means of grace.

The teaching of Vatican II signalled a return to the balanced view of the early Church that the Word of God is proclaimed equally in preaching and in the sacraments. The importance of proclamation is rooted in the nature of Christian faith itself. It is not a human discovery or achievement, but the disclosure of Christ's reconciling work. The priest's responsibility is to proclaim this message of reconciliation to those who have not yet heard it and to win them to faith and to participation in the sacramental life of the Church. Vatican II particularly emphasized the importance of preaching and teaching in opening the hearts and minds of those who receive the sacraments — Baptism, Confirmation, Eucharist, Reconciliation, Matrimony, Anointing and Orders — so that their participation might be as full and fruitful as possible.

In the Christian community itself, especially among those who seem to understand or believe little of what they practise, the preaching of the Word is needed for the very administration of the sacraments. For these are sacraments of faith, and faith is born of the Word and nourished by it. (*Decree on the Ministry and Life of Priests*, section 4)

Preaching is especially important now when faith can no longer be taken for granted. Fewer people come into the Church through birth and custom. Each new church member has to be won from ignorance, indifference or unbelief. Once within the Church his faith has to be sustained and matured through intelligent preaching and teaching. While it is right that Holy Communion should be the focus of Sunday worship, it is a recipe for disaster to relegate the sermon to a subordinate position. There should be sufficient time for sermons that will build up and strengthen faith and understanding.

Effective preaching is not merely the product of the clever application of techniques of communication. Fundamentally it is the outcome of a life dedicated to trying to understand and practise the Christian faith. I have tried to show that preaching must have priority in pastoral work because Christianity is a message to be proclaimed, explained and made intelligible. Consequently it should be recognized on all sides — by parishioners, by diocesan authorities and by parish priests alike — that serious and continuous study of scripture and theology is a fundamental part of ministerial life. Such study is obviously important in all phases of pastoral work, but the quarter of an hour in the pulpit on Sunday morning brings together the fruits of a pastor's life and work.

What is to be looked for in the average preacher is not necessarily a high level of academic expertise, but rather the ability to give a clear and intelligible discourse on the faith which shows both his application to thought and study and his understanding of the needs of his parishioners, gained through pastoral relationships in visiting and counselling.

FURTHER READING

Gordon W. Ireson, *A Handbook of Pastoral Preaching*, Mowbray, 1982.

This is an excellent introduction to the subject; the fruit of a lifetime of teaching and experience.

5 Rite and Sacrament in Pastoral Care

In the opening chapter I showed how the most distinctive feature of pastoral care in Anglo-Catholic parishes was that it was based upon the administration of the rites and sacraments of the Book of Common Prayer. This feature marked a revival in the Church of England of the traditional pattern of Catholic pastoral care. In recent years pastoral care has often been described solely in terms of the personal relationship between pastor and parishioner, but there are now signs of a renewal of an appreciation of the role of rite and sacrament in pastoral work.

In the Roman Catholic Church this has grown out of the revival in liturgical studies and is expressed in the concept of pastoral liturgy. In the United States a number of pastoral theologians, Protestant as well as Catholic, influenced by sociological and anthropological studies of the role of ritual in primitive societies, have looked again at the place of rites and sacraments in the life of the local church. 'Ritual', as a term used by social scientists, has a wider meaning than church ceremonial. It refers to the use of symbolic action in relation to celebrations of important moments in the life of the individual and of society.

Ritual is of particular significance at critical moments in life when a crucial change of status is undergone: at birth, puberty, marriage and death. These rituals, known as the rites of passage, provide socially recognized ways of coping with difficult transitions in life. Typically, a ritual has three phases: separation, transition and re-incorporation. In an African initiation ceremony youths are removed from the village, undergo various testing experiences, and are finally re-incorporated into the community as adults.

Rituals teach through symbol and action, touching levels of consciousness and understanding other than those reached by the verbal and rational. The most important contribution of the Oxford Movement to practical religion was its revival of sacramentalism in a Church where religion had been largely reduced to the verbal. Much that the Anglo-Catholics believed and practised — in religious education, for example — is now out-dated, but their distinctive emphasis upon the centrality of the sacraments is of continuing importance. The Catholic approach to pastoral care, based upon rite and sacrament (in association with preaching, teaching and counselling) appeals to the whole person in a way that more restricted approaches cannot.

However, before examining the practice of pastoral care in relation to the Church's main rites and ceremonies, I will discuss a long-standing pastoral problem associated with the administration of the life-cycle rituals: the failure of most people who use them actively to associate themselves with the Church in any other way.

THE LIFE-CYCLE RITUALS

It is a well-known but puzzling fact that in Britain, as in most Western European countries, although only a small proportion of the population attends Sunday church services frequently and regularly, a much larger proportion uses the rituals of the Church in connection with the key events in life: birth, marriage and death. The issues raised are a constant source of anxiety and debate for the clergy. Let us examine the situation to try to understand it.

About one in every two children born in England is baptized in the Church of England. When baptisms and dedications in the Roman Catholic and Free Churches are also taken into account about four out of every five children are initiated into the Christian Church. About six out of every ten marriages are solemnized in the church of one denomination or another. Of the remaining

26

four civil marriages, at least one involves a divorced person, and it is reasonable to assume that some of these would have married in church had they been able to do so. The undoubted decline in church weddings over the past hundred years is partly accounted for in this way. Although the law does not demand that the committal of a body to burial or cremation has to be accompanied by a service, religious or secular, undertakers assume a minister will officiate. Relatives have to opt out deliberately, and consequently there are very few committals without a religious ceremony.

The churches continue to play a central role in the rituals associated with the crucial turning-points in life: about four in five babies are baptized; about two out of three non-divorced persons marry in church; and virtually everyone is buried or cremated with a religious ceremony.

On the other hand, most estimates put regular church-going at a much lower level, with about one in ten of the adult population in England attending a place of worship each Sunday. Possibly one-quarter of the population attends a Sunday service at least once a month. The Easter communicants of the Church of England represent about one in twenty of the population. The discrepancy between high levels of participation in the life-cycle rituals of the churches and low levels of Sunday church attendance is common (with a few variations) throughout Western Europe. The questions for those engaged in pastoral care centre on why this discrepancy has come about, what it means, and whether it is a transitional state, so that the use of life-cycle rituals will fall off eventually in line with Sunday church attendance.

A common explanation is that non-churchgoers take part in Christian life-cycle rituals not out of conviction (if it were otherwise they would go to church) but because of the continuing influence of custom and tradition. In marrying and having babies baptized in church young couples for whom the faith means nothing are simply responding to parental and family pressures. Undoubtedly these pressures exist and custom and tradition play a large part, but it is also true that many people have a positive desire to be married in church when the alternative of the Register Office exists, and deliberately opt to have their babies baptized when they do not have to. If we admit that custom, tradition, family pressures, the desire to put on a good show and to have a nice setting for the photographs, are all factors but do not add up to a total explanation, what further reasons can we give?

An important difference between the life-cycle rituals and Sunday services is that baptisms, marriages and burials involve family and relatives whereas Parish Communion and Evensong usually do not. The rituals that mark the important transitions of birth, marriage and death symbolize changes in the family and society, and the attendance of relatives and friends is of crucial importance. Also, it is through these rituals that some link between different branches of the family is re-established, an important factor in a society where people move around frequently.

If this is true it provides one explanation why these rituals retain a hold on the allegiance of people who otherwise seem to have little use for the Church. This seems to confirm the suspicion of many parish priests that for the great majority the life-cycle rituals have no religious significance. People, they believe, continue to use these rites because, although bereft of religious meaning for them, they retain a traditional function of holding the family together. The Church is simply the agency performing this function: its religious basis is barely acknowledged.

It is difficult to arrive at a balanced judgement about this. Priests with their theological training are bound to be sceptical of the religious professions of those who rarely, if ever, attend church. Surely to be a Christian involves the worship of God and participation in the sacraments? Whilst this is true, it does not rule out the possiblity of less worked-out and coherent religious beliefs. My experience suggests that those most centrally involved in the life-cycle rituals, the couple, the parents and godparents, do have some religious belief, and what is going on does have some religious significance for them. Atheists and agnostics marry in Register Offices and do not have their babies baptized, but for a large number of people who come to the Church to mark these major occasions, religious symbols and values, which do not impinge on their lives most of the time, take on some significance at a moment of change and emotional upheaval. Young couples often have an imperfectly worked-out feeling that they want to 'do the right thing'. In some sense they affirm belief in the Christian faith. This belief is often incoherent and weakened by doubt and ignorance, but felt strongly in critical moments. Most of the time these beliefs are marginal to their main concerns, but their appearances in church for marriage and baptisms are an affirmation of a desire to continue a link with the Church. This last link is broken where family ties are loose, the Church weak, or where the people concerned belong to a sub-culture which rejects God or marriage (or both); but apparently the mass of the population does not wish to make this break.

FURTHER READING

J.D. Crichton, *Christian Celebration: The Sacraments*, Geoffrey Chapman, 1973

Michael Hocking, *A Handbook of Pastoral Work*, Mowbray, 1977

David Martin, *A Sociology of English Religion*, SCM, 1967

J.D. Crichton's book is a fine example of modern Roman Catholic writing on pastoral liturgy, and is relevant to most of the topics touched on in this book. *The Handbook of Pastoral Work* is the outcome of the writer's long practical experience of pastoral care and shows how in the Anglican Church this is closely bound up with the administration of the sacraments. Martin's work deals with some of the sociological issues touched on in the latter part of this chapter.

6 Christian Initiation

Canon B21 Of Holy Baptism

It is desirable that every minister having a cure of souls shall normally administer the sacrament of Holy Baptism on Sundays at public worship when the most number of people come together, that the congregation there present may witness the receiving of them that be newly baptised into Christ's Church, and be put in remembrance of their own profession made to God in their baptism.

From Canon B22 Of the Baptism Of Infants

1. Due notice, normally of at least a week, shall be given before a child is brought to the church to be baptised.
2. If the minister shall refuse or unduly delay to baptise any such infant, the parents or guardians may apply to the bishop of the diocese, who shall, after consultation with the minister, give such directions as he thinks fit.
3. The minister shall instruct the parents or guardians of an infant to be admitted to Holy Baptism that the same responsibilities rest on them as are in the service of Holy Baptism required of the godparents.
4. No minister shall refuse or, save for the purpose of preparing or instructing the parents or guardians or godparents, delay to baptise any infant within his cure that is brought to the church to be baptised, provided that due notice has been given and the provisions relating to godparents in these Canons are observed.

From Canon B27 Of Confirmation

1. The bishop of every diocese shall himself minister (or cause to be ministered by some other bishop lawfully deputed in his stead) the rite of confirmation throughout his diocese as often and in as many places as shall be convenient, laying his hands upon children and other persons who have been baptised and instructed in the Christian faith.

2. Every minister who has a cure of souls shall diligently seek out children and other persons whom he shall think meet to be confirmed and shall use his best endeavour to instruct them in the Christian faith and life as set forth in the holy Scriptures, the Book of Common Prayer, and the Church Catechism.

3. The minister shall present none to the bishop but such as are come to years of discretion and can say the Creed, the Lord's Prayer, and the Ten Commandments, and can also render an account of their faith according to the said Catechism.

The Canons of the Church of England

BAPTISM AND PASTORAL CARE

New Testament scholars disagree as to whether or not infant Baptism was practised in the early Church, but there is agreement that adult Baptism was the norm for the first few centuries of Christian history. Christian initiation was one rite, made up of three elements: Baptism, Confirmation and first Communion. The rite was preceded by a long period of preparation and testing in the catechumenate. Baptism was the focus both of God's grace and of man's acceptance of the gift of salvation in faith and repentance. It was associated with the remission of sins, the gift of the Holy Spirit, and a new relationship with Christ through the Church.

By the fifth century the norm had shifted from adult to infant Baptism. This was associated with two important developments. One was the idea associated with

31

St Augustine's teaching on original sin, that infants dying un-baptized would not go to heaven. At a time when infant mortality rates were high, this was bound to increase pressure to have babies initiated as soon as possible. The other development was the change from the Church being made up of small groups which grew by converting adults from the alien majority culture, to the Church including all adult members of society, and adding to its numbers by baptizing babies automatically.

From the eighth century, in the West, Confirmation was separated from Baptism. The parish priest baptised the babies but Confirmation was reserved to the bishops, who could only cope with their much-enlarged flocks by confirming children on a different occasion several years later. In the East, the rite of initiation was preserved from dismemberment by the bishops' delegating the power to confirm too, so that infants were baptized, confirmed and communicated for the first time in one rite.

In the West the method of Baptism changed from immersion to infusion (pouring the water on the baby's head). This was accompanied by the use of the Trinitarian formula given at the end of St Mathew's Gospel. Theologians taught that Baptism was necessary to salvation, and that absence of faith in infants was made up for by the presence of the faith of the Church (not even hindered by the unbelief of parents). At Baptism infants received remission of original sin and infusion with grace and virtues. The effects of these gifts showed as the child grew: the power of sin remained, but was weakened, and the child's gifts of grace led to acts of virtue.

At the Reformation, the Church of England retained infant Baptism as its norm. A rite of adult Baptism did not appear in the original sixteenth-century Prayer Books and was added in 1662 only because, in the time of the Commonwealth, Baptist influences had caused some neglect of infant Baptism.

The Oxford Movement strongly reinforced belief in the efficacy of Baptism, and parish priests set out to ensure that all babies were baptized without exception. Infant

Baptism was necessary to salvation; it made it possible to lead a moral life (by weakening the power of sin and infusing virtues) and it made children members of the Church, the source of all grace.

At Wantage W.J. Butler told his curates to note all births and to ensure that Baptism followed. They were to instruct sponsors on their duties, and were to persuade parents to have the service in church, preferably at a public service. Butler was faced with the results of years of pastoral neglect and strong Baptist influence. He made the importance of infant Baptism a strong plank in his teaching, and persuaded those parents who had neglected to do so to have their children baptized. On one occasion five children from a family were baptized together. However, some parents resisted, and he sadly recorded that children died un-baptized. In contrast, he was clearly delighted in 1850 when 'a little girl was baptized, on the second Sunday after her birth, in a service.' This represented his ideal: it was 'very satisfactory for it showed that the true principles of the Church make way with intelligent minds'.

Butler, and thousands of priests like him, far from questioning the baptism of all babies in their parishes, did all they could to bring it about, and taught that it was essential. The situation is now greatly changed and baptismal policy is an urgent pastoral problem. Theologians disagree as to whether or not infant Baptism is theologically justifiable, but even those, including most Roman Catholics and Anglicans, who continue to hold that it is, have grave doubts about traditional practice. I cannot embark on even the beginning of a full discussion of the theological debate, but I will make a couple of points about pastoral practice.

Butler's views were associated with two beliefs now open to question. First, he assumed that all parishioners were, or should be, members of the Church. Now we see the Church as a minority and we can no longer assume the majority are Christians. Second, Butler believed that the un-baptized would not be saved, and it was a burden

33

on his conscience if babies died in that state. This is not a view which commends itself to most of us now. In the light of these two points, it is unlikely that modern pastors will think it right to recruit the babies of non-believers for Baptism in the same way that Butler and other Victorian priests apparently did.

The problem remains of what to do about the request of non-churchgoing parents for a 'christening'. Earlier I suggested that, allowing for the social and other factors involved, these requests may often be associated with residual religious beliefs. St Augustine taught that it did not matter if the parents were unbelievers, for it is the Church's faith that counts, but we are now wary of baptizing if we judge that there is very little hope of the child's receiving a Christian upbringing from its parents.

Two extreme positions on baptismal policy seem to be unacceptable in the Anglican communion: on the one hand, indiscriminate Baptism with no questions asked; on the other refusal to countenance infant Baptism at all. The new rites of the Roman Catholic Church have restored adult Baptism to its earlier position as the norm, but continue to sanction infant Baptism where there is a chance of a Christian upbringing. Many Anglicans would agree with this, but there are difficulties to be faced when a judgement has to be made in particular cases on the possibility of the child's being brought up as a Christian. In my experience refusal to baptize almost always leads to antagonism, rumour and closed doors, as parents feel their child has been rejected by the Church.

When looked at in its historical context, as set out in the first part of this chapter, it can be seen that refusal to baptize marks a drastic reversal of traditional Church policy. In requesting Baptism parents are responding to centuries of Church teaching. This is changing, but time must be allowed for new ideas to be absorbed. In the future it is likely that adult Baptism will become the norm, and infant Baptism is likely to be requested only by parents who actively profess a faith themselves.

Whatever policy is adopted for the present, it is essential

34

that there is thorough preparation for the sacrament. The parents have approached the church, so they are usually prepared to accept instruction. This is best done by a careful study of the service and discussion of the obligations entailed. What the promises involve should be made clear, and this gives the parents the opportunity to back out, if they wish.

Ideally the Baptism should be part of a public service, to symbolize the fact that this is not a private affair but entry into the Church. It reminds the congregation of their obligations towards the child and his family, and also of their own baptisms. The service itself and the sermon should reinforce the teaching given in preparation. After the service it is essential that the pastoral care that has been begun should be followed up so as to help the parents to keep their promises. This is best done, not by the priest alone, but as part of a general parish policy, involving as many church members as possible.

To sum up: in theory at least we appear to be returning to adult Baptism as the norm. In future years as society and the church become more sharply differentiated, Baptism of adult converts who were not baptized as infants will increase in importance, while there is likely to be a decrease in infant baptisms. At the moment the Church has hardly begun to prepare for this: it entails working out how adults will be prepared for Baptism, not just privately by the priest but with the assistance of the whole local church community.

Infant Baptism for the children of believing parents has not been repudiated. It is natural for believers to want their children to be made members of the Church. Infant Baptism witnesses to the fact that Baptism involves not only an act of faith, but also God's saving action. It is not easy to decide where to draw the line between believing and non-believing parents. I have argued that fringe believers will increasingly not bother to request Baptism as the supporting conventions drop away. When they do make such a request I suggest it be taken seriously. It may well be made as a result of some religious awareness, however inadequately expressed. It is essential to give as thorough preparation as possible, leaving it to the parents to decide, in the light of what they have learned, whether to go ahead. Having accepted a child, it is incumbent upon the local church community to do all it can to help parents to nurture it in the Christian faith.

CONFIRMATION

The sacramental teaching of the Oxford Movement led parish priests and bishops to take Confirmation much more seriously than had been the case in the eighteenth century. Special Confirmation classes were introduced in addition to the traditional Sunday catechism classes (they were novel enough in 1850 to be attacked by one parish priest as new-fangled and unnecessary).

At Wantage W.J. Butler saw Christian nurture as a well-ordered progression. The foundation was laid in infancy by Baptism; the basic elements of piety and faith were imparted in the day and Sunday schools; and the process was completed through Confirmation training leading to the sacrament itself.

Butler believed that the laying on of episcopal hands conveyed a special grace of the Holy Spirit to strengthen and perfect the grace of Holy Baptism, empowering recipients to fulfil the vows made for them at Baptism and ratified by them in the first part of the Confirmation service.

At Wantage candidates were divided into separate classes according to age, ability and social status. Each class met twice a week over a six-week period from early November to mid-December. Assuming that the candidates knew the catechism by heart, had acquired a basic knowledge of the Bible, and had established the habit of daily prayer, Butler lectured them on 'definite theology' (including the doctrines of God, creation, original sin, the atonement, the sacraments, and concluding with an account of the new life Christ brings and 'keeping the commandments'). He attempted to relate his teaching to the practical application of the Christian life in relation to morals and the sacraments. At the end of each lecture he questioned his class closely to discover what had been understood and retained.

In addition to the dozen sessions with each class, Butler interviewed the candidates individually. In 1863 there were 67. Butler used the interviews to discuss rules of life (in 1863 he noted a 'sad lack of prayer') and moral questions (in 1865 two girls were denied Confirmation because of 'their bad characters'. Boys were warned against 'the sins of the flesh').

Butler's diocesan bishop was Samuel Wilberforce of Oxford. He had been influenced by the ideals of the Oxford Movement and was anxious to co-operate with the parish clergy in making Confirmation services reverent and memorable occasions. Each December he travelled to Wantage and did all he could to impress the candidates with the solemnity of the occasion.

At Wantage there was a three-week gap between the Confirmation service and the candidates' first Communion. Butler used these weeks to give special preparation classes. He regarded it as 'delicate work' requiring great tact, for the candidates were often fearful, shy and ignorant. In 1864 he had 'a long conversation with W' who he hoped would become a communicant, but W shrank from taking this step and Butler concluded that this was due to his 'early upbringing, which filled his mind with prejudices'. In 1864 he reckoned that 'at least 22 out of the 37 candidates would become communicants.'

The pattern established at Wantage and elsewhere in Anglo-Catholic parishes has continued, with modifications, to the present day. Nowadays a course may well continue over a longer period, although rarely twice a week as at Wantage, and there is less of a gap (or no gap at all) between Confirmation and first Communion. But whereas Butler took the rightness of the pattern for granted, for us it raises a host of questions both practical and theological.

During the first centuries of Christian history Confirmation was administered as part of an integral rite of Christian initiation. Following a long period of preparation adults received Baptism, Confirmation and first Communion on one occasion. When infant Baptism became the norm, Confirmation became a separate rite in the Western Church. Babies were baptized as soon as possible by their parish priests, but a number of years elapsed before the bishop came to confirm them. In the Eastern Church Baptism, Confirmation and first Communion were all administered in infancy. During the Middle Ages Western theologians rationalized the changed practice of initiation by stating that Confirmation represented a separate strengthening by the Holy Spirit. The Reformation Church of England was influenced by the Protestant view that Confirmation was primarily a rite of personal commitment.

Recent Roman Catholic liturgical revisions have re-established the unified rite of Christian initiation for adults as the norm. However, at the moment this is an ideal, for in the Roman, as in the Anglican, communion the later separate Confirmation of those baptized in infancy remains the general practice.

In 1976 the General Synod of the Church of England decided against changing the current practice of confirming children baptized in infancy when they 'are come to years of discretion' (Canon B27, section 3). This is unsatisfactory in that it splits Baptism and Confirmation when it is widely agreed that they should be reunited. Also, it is difficult to believe that young adolescents have reached 'years of discretion' when so many of them lapse from the communicant life soon after beginning. One solution which has much to commend it is that the two elements associated with Confirmation, the gift of the Holy Spirit and personal commitment, should be split in the case of those baptized in infancy, the first element to be reunited with Baptism, and the second to be made at a much later date when a truly free and personal commitment could be made.

Meanwhile, parishes have to do their best in the present anomalous situation. I conclude by describing a imaginative scheme called 'The Quest', devised in the ecumenical parish of Swindon Old Town, and intended as a radical experiment in Confirmation training. It started from the premise that the traditional scheme of preparation over a limited period of months was too short and too often preoccupied with the needs of the one event of Confirmation. Instead Confirmation training was inserted into a wider scheme of preparation for Christian life extending over the three years which take the young person from puberty, at about thirteen, to young adulthood at seventeen. Opportunities for Confirmation are offered during the course, but it is made clear that there is a completely free decision to be made about this, and it is possible to continue without opting for Confirmation. The emphasis on continuity also helps to overcome the frequent criticism of conventional arrangements that they make Confirmation a 'passing-out' parade after which the young think they have done all that is necessary, and fail to attend post-Confirmation classes or even Holy Communion.

The Quest scheme also attempts to involve as many church members as possible. Each of the three years of the course has its own leader, secretary and team. Much is made of learning by activity and involvement. The first two years include residential weekends, and a number of visits to widen experience. The young people undertake some form of service to the community, such as hospital visiting, and they go to London to see examples of the Church's work in various kinds of social action.

The virtue of this scheme is that it provides a progressive programme of preparation for Christian life. It does not make Confirmation the be-all and end-all, and it would retain its relevance if present Confirmation practices were changed. It maximizes the use of lay talents, and its teaching methods are not merely academic but suited to the needs and abilities of all types of young people. It is a good example of what can be achieved with planning and the co-operation of priest and laity.

FURTHER READING

J.D. Crichton, *Christian Celebration: The Sacraments*, Geoffrey Chapman, 1973

A.T. Hanson and R.P.C. Hanson, *Reasonable Belief*, Oxford University Press, 1980

D. Palmer, *Quest*, Ecumenical Parish of Swindon Old Town, 1975

Crichton discusses pastoral practice in relation to recent developments in theology. The Hansons summarize recent theological developments in a chapter on 'Christian Initiation'.

7 Teaching the Faith

Canon B26 Of Teaching the Young

1. Every minister shall take care that the children and young people within his cure are instructed in the doctrine, sacraments, and discipline of Christ, as the Lord has commanded and as they are set forth in the holy Scriptures, in the Book of Common Prayer, and especially in the Church Catechism; and to this end he, or some godly and competent persons appointed by him, shall on Sundays or if need be at other convenient times diligently instruct and teach them in the same.

2. All parents and guardians shall take care that their children receive such instruction.

The Canons of the Church of England

ANGLO-CATHOLICS AND THE RELIGIOUS INSTRUCTION OF CHILDREN

Nineteenth-century Anglo-Catholics had a clear idea of the purpose of education: it was to instil the moral and religious beliefs of the Church of England. These beliefs, revealed by God and presented in Scripture, were to be taught by the Church with God's authority. From the 1840s onwards all good parish priests ensured that there were Church schools in their parishes, their chief aim being to teach the faith of the Church. The parish priest demonstrated this aim symbolically by taking charge as chief manager and teacher of the school, opening and closing the school day with prayer, imparting daily religious instruction, and generally impressing his personal influence upon the pupils. A new profession of school teacher was emerging from the training colleges, but it was subordinated to the priest in order to demonstrate the inferiority of mere intellectual training to moral and religious instruction. It was suggested that even arithmetic lessons might teach moral truths: a class might add up how much a drunkard wastes in a year, for example. It was also suggested that too much emphasis was placed on training children to read and write. The only acceptable reason for teaching the poor to read was to enable them to study the Bible.

Even this was not necessary because God had saved millions of illiterates. The Christian life was based upon moral rather than intellectual knowledge and could be learned without reading books.

Anglo-Catholics were firmly opposed to the rising demand for literacy and rational knowledge. They were interested only in what led to salvation: worldly knowledge counted for nothing; or, even worse, it led men astray from the pursuit of the one thing needful, the holy life. But if there was a battle on against the growing demands for secular education, there was also a long-standing battle against popular ignorance of the Christian faith.

Anglo-Catholics complained constantly that the mass of people were ignorant of Christian doctrine, morality and worship. They regarded baptism as a registration ceremony: they had no idea of its sacramental value as a means of regeneration and grace. To them Holy Communion was the reserve of the pious and the dying. They regarded it as a source of religious feelings and not as a channel of grace. They had no idea of Christian doctrines, merely holding a vague belief in God. Although they acknowledged Christian morality in general terms they failed to observe it in relation to sexual morality, for it was common for brides from the labouring classes to be pregnant.

The common solution to the two problems, the inroads of secular education and popular ignorance of the faith, was to increase parochial education, with dogmatic teaching

42

as its aim. The method to be used was the catechetical method of the Church.

Anglo-Catholics greatly valued the use of the catechism of the Book of Common Prayer, not merely because it had authority, but also because of what were believed to be its educational and religious values. It was an active method of teaching and learning, consisting of questions and answers which forced the pupils to think and to express their thoughts. When it was conducted in church as laid down in the Prayer Book the children were imbued 'with the solemnity of the place', and the parents would witness and be involved in their children's education and learn something themselves.

Most important of all, the catechism was esteemed in Anglo-Catholic circles because it embodied the 'Catholic' view of religious education in being dogmatic and aimed at inciting devotion. For, although it proceeded on a question and answer basis, the answers were already there in the book to be learned. They were the answers of the Church: clear dogmatic and final. There was a strong moral element: learning the catechism entailed learning the Ten Commandments. Both of these elements, doctrine and morals, were presented dogmatically but not abstractly, for they were presented in the context of worship. When taxed with queries about the ability of young children to understand the abstract concepts of the catechism, Anglo-Catholics replied that they were 'learned through devotion'. Grace worked at a deeper level than intellect, enabling the assimilation of truths otherwise beyond the reach of rational understanding.

The Anglo-Catholics taught that school education had a specific aim, that an increase of it in its Catholic form was urgent, and that there was a Catholic method, but how and where was it to take place?

So far we have mentioned the parochial schools which appeared in increasing numbers from the 1840s onwards. These were to be the focus, but they were never a complete solution. Up to the 1880s school was not compulsory, so some children hardly went at all, many disappeared at harvest time, and most left by about the age of ten. Further, the Church was unable to afford to build sufficient schools. From 1870 onwards the inadequate provision of church schools was increasingly overshadowed by state provision, and in the new Board schools catechetical teaching was specifically forbidden. Anglo-Catholics campaigned against non-denominational biblical teaching, but without success.

There were various attempts to supplement the inadequacies of the parochial school. The Sunday School movement which had rapidly developed from the 1780s onwards was adapted to Anglo-Catholic needs. Parish priests would have children meeting in church on Sunday afternoons to learn Church teaching given by voluntary helpers under supervision. But there were constant complaints that Sunday Schools tended to become self-contained institutions with little graduation to full church membership. So many priests continued with the tradition of catechizing in church on Sunday.

In addition, from the 1840s onwards the new institution of Confirmation classes became widely accepted. These were to be the culmination of the Christian nurture of the young: the foundation was laid in Baptism (nothing could be learned without grace), the rudiments of faith and piety were instilled in the day and Sunday schools, and the Confirmation class completed the process by leading to complete self-dedication and the communicant life.

RELIGIOUS EDUCATION TODAY

Religious education in the modern British state school is very different from the scripture or religious instruction lessons of the Victorian era, or even from the practice of just twenty years ago. Anglo-Catholics assumed that day schools were part of the parochial system of pastoral care. As agents of the Church their aim was to teach the faith and practice of the Catholic Church as interpreted by the Church of England. The main method of teaching was that which had the Church's authority, the catechetical method. The content of the catechism was a summary of the doctrines and morals of the Church. The hoped-for outcome of teaching was not mere knowledge but personal religious practice in terms of worship, participation in the sacraments, and holiness of life. Religious teaching was imparted, not merely in special subject lessons, but through prayer and worship and the whole ethos of the school.

These high ideals survived only in a minority of schools in the early twentieth century. The majority of schools had the more limited aim of teaching scripture without reference to church doctrine, together with a little church history. This arrangement was the outcome of a compromise which allowed religious teaching to continue in state schools by limiting it to what was believed to be a common denominator betweeen the rival interpretations of the Church of England and the Free Churches. This compromise was very different from the American solution of the same problem. Under the terms of the United States constitution, religious education was excluded from public (state) schools. Consequently much more was done to develop the educational facilities of the churches themselves.

The compromise of 1870 marked the effective end of the Church of England's pretension to be the sole educator of the nation and sole source of religious teaching. It was now in effect one denomination among a number of competing religious groups. But the compromise preserved the assumption that England was a Christian country in which it was proper for the nation's schools to inculcate the national faith. This assumption was questioned only by small minority secularist groups in the Victorian and Edwardian periods. In the early 1900s a small Moral Instruction League tried, unsuccessfully, to promote moral education as a substitute for religious teaching. But for the most part religious instruction was not widely questioned, even if it was rarely accorded an important place in schools.

A major landmark in English educational history was the 1944 Education Act. Passed towards the end of a war fought in defence of Christian civilization, when thoughts were turning to post-war reconstruction, the Act deliberately laid it down that the school day should begin with an act of worship and that religious instruction should be given to all pupils. The post-war years saw the publication of a number of religious instruction syllabuses, still centred on biblical studies together with a little Church history. One development was the incorporation of the results of the critical study of the Bible. School biblical study conformed to the dominant pattern in university theological departments with their concentration on historical critical studies of the scriptures.

In the 1960s the inherited pattern of religious education came in for criticism. A small but articulate humanist movement, with a sizeable proportion of its membership in the teaching profession, forcefully questioned the hitherto largely unquestioned scheme of teaching the Christian faith. Also Christian educationalists such as Harold Loukes and Ronald Goldman raised questions about the effectiveness of current biblical teaching.

At the beginning of the next decade a Schools Council Working Paper on Religious Education in Secondary Schools argued that the traditional pattern, labelled as the 'confessional approach', was no longer legitimate in a pluralist society where people held a variety of beliefs or none, and that the aim of the state school should be limited to helping pupils to understand religion. This would entail the study of more than one religion and exclude any attempt to induct pupils into a particular faith. As well as the study of 'explicit' religion, the beliefs and institutions of particular faiths, there should also be the study of 'implicit' religion, encompassing those aspects of experience, feelings of mystery and awe, the study of which helped in an understanding of religion.

CATECHESIS

Victorian Anglo-Catholics assigned a key role to religion in school, untroubled about the problems associated with imposing instruction upon all. Today most schools are independent of church control. The result of the shift in religious teaching in schools from the ideal of induction into a basic form of Christian faith to a more neutral attempt to teach an understanding of religion is that, except where there is a church school, the Church has become the sole source of Christian nurture, apart from any training given by parents.

Church-based religious education differs from that of the state school in being focused upon worship. The heart of the life of the parish church is the worship of God; induction of the young into that life must include, and go beyond, learning about scripture and Christian belief, and lead them to worship itself. This kind of religious education is usefully called 'catechesis' to distinguish it from 'religious education' which is usually the term used in schools. The use of the term catechesis does not imply that the Church's work in initiating children into an understanding of Christian Faith is not based upon educational principles, but its use does imply that the aim is to go beyond the limits of school-based religious education, to personal commitment and worship.

Religious education provides a foundation for catechesis. 'Implicit' religious education uncovers experiences of awe, wonder, mystery and love, as a basis for understanding the place of these emotions in religion. Catechists may see these experiences as forms of awareness of God. 'Explicit' religious education leads to a knowledge of religious beliefs and practices and to an appreciation of the nature of religion and its role in life. Where religious education has been given sympathetically and well, it provides a basis for the Church to build on.

Modern religious education also helps catechists to improve their work as educationalists. All phases of pastoral care involve the use of ideas and methods drawn from current psychological and educational practice. Attempts to retain 'traditional' methods often mean that the Church simply preserves secular methods of the past. The second Vatican Council in several of its documents

47

recommends the use of modern methods of pastoral care, drawn from the social and human sciences. This advice is repeated in the recent Roman Catholic *Catechist's Handbook* which lays down that 'The church encourages the use of the biological, social and psychological sciences in pastoral care.'

In Victorian times Roman and Anglo-Catholics identified the idea of catechesis with the use of the formal written catechism, a product of the Reformation. Luther devised a catechism, as a summary of Christian teaching in question and answer form, in order to try to improve knowledge of the faith. His success led Anglicans and Roman Catholics to follow suit. In time it came to be thought of as *the* catechetical method. However, it was merely the product of one era of Christian history, embodying educational methods which are now out-dated.

Its method was deductive. Children were taught general principles and then expected to apply these abstract principles to particular circumstances. For a long time now educationalists have emphasized the importance of inductive methods which start from concrete experiences. 'The inductive approach proceeds from the sensible, visible, tangible experiences of the person, and leads, with the help of the Holy Spirit, to more general conclusions and principles' (*A Catechist's Handbook* 1980, p.108).

Another important aspect of modern educational thought is the explanation of the various phases of in-tellectual, moral and emotional development. Intellectual and moral development do not proceed simply in terms of quantity, the acquisition of more and more knowledge, but qualitative changes in conceptual and moral thinking take place. Children take a long time to acquire the ability to think in terms of abstract concepts, and pass through preliminary stages dominated by intuitive or concrete modes of thought. Similarly, the ability to make free moral decisions for oneself is arrived at, if at all, only after passing through various phases of obedience to authority and conformity to conventional norms.

Education takes place only when the child understands

what he has been taught. Children can appear to learn in obedience to authority or by parroting answers, but that is not education. True education requires that learners understand and think critically about what they have been told. Victorian Anglo-Catholics taught dogmatically that their views alone were true, and their audiences were expected to accept this passively without dissent. Our task is to teach with conviction and yet at the same time encourage critical thought and discussion. Christians constantly find their beliefs questioned; they have to be helped not to be afraid of criticism and to have reasons for the faith that is in them.

However, as Victorian Anglo-Catholics understood, catechesis goes beyond intellectual education. Its aim is to lead to mature faith and to build up a sense of Christian identity. As well as teaching about Scripture and belief, it is also concerned with Christian practice in prayer, worship and the care of others. Children of junior school age are at a stage when their basic attitudes are being formed, and should be fully integrated into the worshipping life of the Church. Leslie Francis's book *His Spirit is With Us* provides an excellent scheme for this purpose.

ADULT EDUCATION

In Victorian times vigorous attempts were made to improve the religious education of adults. Evangelicals instituted Bible study groups, while Anglo-Catholics held communicant classes.

W.J. Butler's communicant classes at Wantage were nationally famous. One observer described them as 'the mainstay of the whole work' in the parish. After Confirmation Butler shepherded his communicants into groups which each met once a month. Like the Confirmation classes, these groups were selected according to age, sex and social class. There were seven categories: young ladies; young men; young women; older married women; older choir lads; labourers; and pupil teachers. He had between 150 and 300 people attending in at least seven classes. He received each classs at the vicarage and addressed them in 'a conversational rather than a sermonizing tone'. The topic of the address usually related to some aspect of the communicant life. The hour ended with prayer, and he made it possible for individuals to stay afterwards for personal advice and instruction.

In recent years, as is evident in Roman Catholic catechetical literature, there has been a shift of emphasis in church education. Without minimizing the importance of the education and nurture of children, the ultimate aim is seen to be the promotion of maturity of faith in adults. One main reason for this is apparent from our earlier discussion of changes in church and society. When the Church operated in a society in which the truth of Christianity was assumed and religious practice was conventional, a basic minimum level of belief and practice was maintained by social convention alone. Now the position is reversed: it is conventional to be apathetic or unbelieving and to ignore religious practice. Most people are socialized into a non-religious way of life by apathetic or non-believing parents. Just as in the past the atheist had to make a conscious and courageous effort to defy convention in the name of principle, so now the Christian has to make a conscious stand against irreligious conformity.

What we believe to be the truth is not something we think up simply by ourselves. We learn it from others, particularly those close to us. We tend to take their account of the world and their values for granted. In this situation the local church has to take positive action to counteract the corroding influence of non-Christian beliefs and values.

Whereas in the nineteenth century adult religious education was largely devotional, it is now much wider in scope and content. As an example of this I shall conclude this brief discussion with an account of a course organized by the Training Council of the Board of Education of the Diocese of Rochester.

First run in 1979, the 'Foundation Course' is seen as 'a diocesan training course for church members'. It is made up of separate units on the Old and New Testaments;

50

Christian belief and practice; Church history; liturgy and worship; prayer; ecumenism; human relationships; the Christian and work; the Christian and society; and the Church and other faiths. Each unit is prepared by a team of clerical and lay consultants and is taught one evening a week for six or seven weeks by trained tutors with groups of about a dozen members in centres throughout the diocese.

The year is divided into three terms and it is hoped that participants will take one unit a term, so covering six units over two years and qualifying for a Diocesan Certificate. This is seen for some as a first step towards further training as priests, readers, or pastoral workers; but for most it is an end in itself.

This course is an example of adult religious education planned on a diocesan scale, although operated in a number of centres for members of the local deanery or parish. As well as commanding greater resources, such a scheme emphasizes that the local church belongs to a movement whose message transcends local loyalties. Earlier I mentioned the importance of the local church, but there is a need to counteract inward-looking tendencies by showing that the church community is more than a club in that its primary purpose is its commitment to the life and teachings of Jesus Christ.

FURTHER READING

Leslie Francis, *His Spirit is With Us:A Project Approach to Christian Nurture*, Collins, 1981

Nora Hanlon, *Heirs to the Kingdom:Catechesis for Children*, St Paul Publications, 1980

Incorporated Catholic Truth Society, *A Catechist's Handbook*, CTS, 1980

D.J.O'Leary and T. Sallnow, *Love and Meaning in Religious Education*, Oxford, 1982

Kevin Nichols, *Cornerstone*, St Paul Publications, 1978

Kevin Nichols and John Cummins, *Into His Fulness: Adult Religious Education Today*, St Paul Publications, 1980

Angela Tilby, *Teaching God*, Collins, 1979

Cornerstone is a clear introduction to modern Roman Catholic catechetical ideas. It is the first of a series of which *Heirs to the Kingdom* and *Into His Fulness* are the second and third volumes. *A Catechist's Handbook* is a useful survey of the field. *Love and Meaning in Religious Education* is a more advanced work than those so far mentioned, but is important in that it roots religious education in theology (notably that of Karl Rahner). *His Spirit is With Us* is an important Anglican attempt to provide a course for children of junior school age with the aim of integrating them into the worshipping life of the church. *Teaching God* is a lively and critical account of current trends in religious education.

8 The Pastoral Care of Marriage

Canon B30 Of Holy Matrimony

1. The Church of England affirms, according to our Lord's teaching, that marriage is in its nature a union permanent and life-long, for better for worse, till death them do part, of one man with one woman, to the exclusion of all others on either side, for the procreation and nurture of children, for the hallowing and right direction of the natural instincts and affections, and for the mutual society, help and comfort which the one ought to have of the other, both in prosperity and adversity.

2. The teaching of our Lord affirmed by the Church of England is expressed and maintained in the Form of Solemnisation of Matrimony contained in the Book of Common Prayer.

3. It shall be the duty of the minister, when application is made to him for matrimony to be solemnised in the church of which he is the minister, to explain to the two persons who desire to be married the Church's doctrine of marriage as herein set forth, and the need of God's grace in order that they may discharge aright their obligations as married persons.

The Canons of the Church of England

CHANGING VIEWS OF MARRIAGE

Victorian parish priests have left detailed accounts of their pastoral care of the sick and dying, indicating their sense of the priority of this aspect of their work. In contrast, their parish diaries and lectures on pastoral work said virtually nothing about marriage. There were grumbles about the immorality of the lower orders, attacks on Register Offices and legislation allowing divorce, but little else. Although they read banns and performed marriage services, they seem to have taken this aspect of ministry for granted.

In the twentieth century marriage has become a central concern for pastoral care because the Christian ideal of marriage, taken for granted one hundred years ago even by those who failed to live up to it, is now questioned and undermined. In Victorian times divorce was rare and frowned upon; now it is commonplace and socially acceptable. The effect of increasingly permissive legislation is that divorce is now widely accepted as the obvious recourse when a marriage goes wrong. As a consequence the Christian belief in lifelong, permanent and monogamous marriage is widely disregarded.

In the light of this situation, and of the more positive consideration that modern men and women have a higher ideal of marriage, there has developed a desire to enhance pastoral care in this sphere. About two-thirds of all marriages take place in churches (about four in ten in Anglican churches), and the clergy who conduct these ceremonies have a duty to help couples both to understand what they are doing in entering into Christian marriage, and also to fulfil the promises they make.

This is not the place for a detailed discussion of the moral theology of marriage or for debates on Christian ethics about divorce and contraception, but I shall state briefly what I understand to be some of the key features of Christian teaching in the light of scripture and of recent church pronouncements, notably the Pastoral Constitution on the Church in Modern World issued by the Second Vatican Council.

THE CHURCH'S VIEW

What the Church has to say about marriage grows out of

its basic teaching about the nature of God and his relationship with man. In recent years, without repudiating the traditional view that the 'end' of marriage is to produce children, an equal emphasis has been given to the personal relationship between the couple. This was expressed clearly by the Second Vatican Council. 'Marriage to be sure is not instituted solely for procreation. Rather, its very nature as an unbreakable compact between persons, and the welfare of children, both demand that the mutual love of the spouses, too, be embodied in a rightly ordered manner, that it grow and ripen.' (Pastoral Constitution on the Church in the Modern World, p. 50)

The bishops cited a number of scriptural passages to support their statement that 'The biblical Word of God several times urges the betrothed and the married to nourish and develop their wedlock by pure conjugal love and undivided affection' (p. 49). They also acknowledged that the source of the Church's deeper understanding of this aspect of marriage was not only scripture but also modern thought. 'Many men of our own age also highly regard true love between husband and wife' (p. 49).

Although the recent Christian emphasis upon marriage as essentially a personal relationship is rooted in scriptural teaching, it also owes a debt to modern insights into human relationships, notably those of psychology. These new ideas clarify what is meant by love in Christian marriage. 'This love is an eminently human one since it is directed from one person to another through an affection of the will. It involves the good of the whole person.' It is out-going, self-giving, directed towards the other person. This kind of love 'leads the spouses to a free and mutual gift of themselves, a gift proving itself by gentle affection and by deed.'

The modern Christian emphasis in explaining the nature of the marriage bond is upon the idea of marriage as a convenant. The Pastoral Constitution follows on from its discussion of love in marriage by linking it with this idea. 'Christ the Lord abundantly blessed this many-faceted love, welling up as it does from the foundation of divine

55

love and structured as it is on the model of His union with the Church. For as God of old made Himself present to His people through a covenant of love and fidelity, so now the Saviour of men and the Spouse of the Church comes into the lives of married Christians through the sacrament of matrimony' (p. 48). The new covenant was made between God and the Church through Jesus Christ. The sacraments (including marriage) are ways in which Christ is active in the lives of believers, so in the covenant of marriage Christ is present to husband and wife. 'He abides with them thereafter so that, just as He loved the Church and handed Himself over on her behalf, the spouses may love each other with perpetual fidelity through mutual self-bestowal' (p. 48).

This emphasis upon marriage as a covenant relationship, in which husband and wife pledge faithfulness to each other in the light of God's pledged faithfulness to them, leads us to understand Jesus' teaching on the permanence of marriage. It affirms that permanent, lifelong, monogamous marriage was God's creation. It is not laying down a law nor an impossible moral ideal, but affirming the nature of marriage as a covenant in which the couple pledge to each other for life. It is difficult to see how an intention to pledge mutual self-giving love can be other than an unconditional commitment for life.

For most people marriage represents the most important relationship of their lives. A major pastoral problem is to show how Christian teaching relates to the concerns of ordinary everyday life. Marriage affords the Church an opportunity to demonstrate the practical relevance of its teaching on love to the needs of married couples. This is not to say that the Church should endorse all modern views on marriage: it is arguable that excessively high and unrealistic ideals of marriage are themselves a contributory factor in marital breakdown. Jesus taught that marriage is not our ultimate concern, for that is God, and that there will be no marriages in heaven. But even given a sober and realistic appraisal of the place of marriage, it must still be argued that a major responsibility of the local church today is to develop its work in relation to the pastoral care of marriage. Vatican II laid it down that:

> It devolves on priests duly trained about family matters to nurture the vocation of spouses by a variety of pastoral means, by preaching God's word, by liturgical worship, and by other spiritual aids to family and conjugal life; to sustain them sympathetically and patiently in difficulties, and to make them courageous through love (Pastoral Constitution on the Church in the Modern World, section 52).

PREPARATION FOR MARRIAGE

An important aspect of this is the preparation of couples who come seeking marriage in church. Marriage, like the other occasional services, presents an important pastoral opportunity to explain the Christian faith and its application. One way is to discuss with the couple what they think marriage is for, leading on to a study of the text of the service where the Church's teaching is set forth. It is important that they see the service as a public act of worship and understand something of what worship is. What can be done in a few interviews is limited. Most couples will be non-churchgoers, not out of hostility to the Church but because of social conditioning. It is possible to help them to participate more fully in the service by guiding them to understand something of its meaning, and to see the Church, not as something remote, but as a community of people to whom they may turn in the future for help.

THE MARRIAGE SERVICE

The service itself is the central act of pastoral care in relation to marriage. In it the Church helps the couple to make the transition from one state of life as single persons to a new state as married persons. The words, the symbols and the actions of the service transmit the beliefs and

57

values of the Church. The service is not private but a public act of worship in which, as well as the couple directly concerned, the unmarried learn something of the Christian idea of marriage, and the already married are reminded of the vows, ideals and values with which they began. If the service is to succeed in teaching and helping these various people then it has to be carefully prepared and conducted.

The introduction to the service sets out some basic themes: marriage was instituted by God and it is good; it signifies the covenant between Christ and the Church; it is for the procreation of children, and for mutual love. The scripture reading, preferably chosen and studied by the couple beforehand, together with the address, builds on these themes.

The priest in asking the man and woman if they will love each other implies that this is an act of will, a commitment of the whole self, and that love is not a mere transient feeling. The gift of the bride emphasizes that her parents recognize that she now belongs to a new family. Failure to respect this damages or even destroys a marriage. The vows are the heart of the matter: the couple pledge to each other lifelong faithfulness. The meaning of Christian marriage is made clear in these words, in the action of holding hands and in the symbol of the ring(s).

The concluding prayers affirm the joy of Christian marriage and call upon the resources of God's grace for the couple to match the promises they have made. Ideally these prayers will be caught up in the eucharistic prayer in which the covenant between Christ and believer, the basis of marriage, is strengthened and renewed.

FURTHER READING

The literature on the pastoral care of marriage is extremely extensive. The National Marriage Guidance Council, Little Church Street, Rugby, issues comprehensive bibliographies on marriage and counselling. Dr Jack Dominian, a Roman Catholic psychiatrist, who specializes in the subject, has written a number of helpful books. A recent work is J. Dominian, *Marriage, Faith and Love*, Darton, Longman and Todd, 1981. Another Roman Catholic writer I have found illuminating is Walter Kasper, *The Theology of Christian Marriage*, Burns and Oates, 1980.

9 Visiting and Counselling

From Canon C24 Of Priests Having a Cure of Souls

6. He shall be diligent in visiting his parishioners, particularly those who are sick and infirm; and he shall provide opportunities whereby any of his parishioners may resort unto him for spiritual counsel and advice.

The Canons of the Church of England

VISITING

A characteristic feature of the Anglican pastoral tradition is an emphasis upon the value of visiting parishioners in their homes. Some who question its value suggest that it was merely a Victorian invention, but Chaucer's reference to the practice of the poor country priest in the Prologue to the Canterbury Tales suggests that it originated before the Reformation. Although Chaucer's priest's parish was 'wide . . . with houses asunder', he 'neglected not in rain or thunder' to call on those 'in sickness or in trouble'. Nearly three centuries later, Herbert's Country Parson 'visited upon the afternoons in the weekdays . . . now one quarter of the parish, now another'. There he would find 'his flock most naturally in midst of their affairs'. He blessed the house on arrival and then taught the family about the Christian faith and its duties. He asked 'what order [was] kept in the house about prayers mornings and evenings on their knees, reading of scripture, catechising, singing of psalms at work and on holy days.' He also encouraged and helped with teaching the children to read, and made a point of visiting the cottages of the poor to open 'not only his mouth, but his purse to their relief'.

Visiting was high on the list of the duties of the Victorian parson. W.J. Butler told his Wantage curates that 'no task was more important than the duty of regular home visiting.' He expected them to put in four hours a day, for 'unremitting visiting [was] the real secret of keeping a parish well in hand.' There was 'nothing more true than the old saying "a house-going Parson makes a churchgoing people".'

A distinction was made between visitation of the sick and dying, which took priority, and general visiting. With the sick there was a clear purpose to the visit, but when there was no obvious aim it was difficult to steer the conversation to the subject of 'personal religion'. People were reluctant to admit to being sinners needing spiritual help. Nevertheless, Butler was convinced that visiting was 'the only method' of raising the spiritual level of parish life. It made it possible to open the heart of the individual in a way which could not 'be effected by sermons and mass affairs'.

George Herbert had fewer than 1000 parishioners to deal with. W.J. Butler had more than three or four times as many, but always had one or two curates to help. Today most parish priests are single-handed and often have to cope with huge urban populations or a number of scattered rural parishes. The fact that people move far more frequently than they used to do adds to the problem. Often the wife as well as the husband is out for most of the day, and television programmes fill the evening hours. Not only is it usually impossible to visit more than a fraction of the total number of people in the parish; it is often difficult to arrange to see even those who appear to need a visit.

Parishioners often have unrealistic expectations in this respect. Priests have a clear duty to visit the sick and the dying, and most priests are grateful to be told when someone is dying. Then there will be visits in connection with baptisms, confirmations, marriages and funerals. All of these have a purpose, and form part of a continuing process of care. In any sizable parish these, together with visits to people in special difficulty, will take up a considerable amount of the time the priest has for visiting. Some may have time for more general visiting, and the Anglican priest is still welcome in many homes. Systematic visiting of the homes of non-churchgoers is probably best arranged as a joint task by the whole church community. Of particular value is the practice of having a church representative in each street, who can call on newcomers and advise the priest of those who need or would like a visit.

COUNSELLING

The traditional use of the term 'counsel' was in connection with a consultation between lawyer and client, or priest and parishioner. A problem was presented for solution and advice was given on the basis of knowledge and experience. The modern idea of counselling is based on psychology and the therapeutic interview. Whereas the lawyer or priest gave authoritative advice, much modern counselling has been based on a non-authoritarian approach. In recent years Christian pastoral care has been influenced by the new ideas and methods, a development which has produced a wide range of reactions, from enthusiastic welcome to hostile rejection.

There are many schools of counselling, and recently attempts have been made to assess the usefulness of various approaches. This research has shown that two approaches seem to show consistent evidence of success, and there also appears to be agreement that certain qualities in the counsellor are more important for helpful counselling than any particular theories or methods.

The two approaches showing therapeutic value are the non-directive approach, pioneered by Carl Rogers, and therapies, based on psychological studies of the principles of social learning. No one approach seems to be sufficient in itself, but in combination they make a useful contribution to effective counselling. A number of recent books on counselling agree on a three-stage model which puts together elements of the different approaches.

The first element is usually based upon the idea of non-directive counselling. The counsellor sets out to establish and maintain a supportive relationship with his client: he tries to convey that what is told is accepted and not judged. By careful listening he tries to enter into the thoughts and feelings of the other person in order to understand him. He shows respect and consideration, and a genuine concern for his client. By showing non-possessive warmth, he enables the client to express himself freely. This careful listening may be sufficient to help a person who needs simply to unburden himself of anxieties and fears. The listening is not merely passive, but an active attempt to put oneself alongside a troubled person.

A second element, and possibly a third, may be needed in the counselling relationship. The second element is a more active attempt to help the client to clarify his problem, by exploring with him points raised earlier. The third element enters when a counsellor takes a more directive role: giving advice, or suggesting further help is needed from, for example, a doctor.

It may appear that counselling has come full circle, back to the old ideas of authoritative advice-giving. This, however, would be to ignore the fact that most recent 'eclectic' models of counselling retain, as a fundamental basis, the insights of the non-directive approach. This approach is not entirely new: spiritual directors in the past listened carefully to what was said to them and tried to understand the individual needs and experiences of those who came to them, before making judgements or giving advice. Nevertheless, psychological approaches like that of Carl Rogers have been of value in reminding pastors of the need to listen and to understand before offering guidance.

Recent studies of counselling have reaffirmed that the most important element in effective counselling is the counsellor's own personal qualities and attitudes. More important than methods of counselling, or theories of personality development, are the counsellor's genuine concern, his non-possessive warmth, and his ability to enter imaginatively into another's feelings, that is, to empathize. These qualities provide the primary supportive element in modern counselling.

So far I have discussed ideas about counselling developed in the fields of psychotherapy and social work. In recent years attempts have been made to adapt these approaches to the service of Christian pastoral care. It is now widely accepted that the practice of non-directive counselling, described as the basic element in most contemporary models of counselling, can help to improve pastoral relationships. If it does nothing else, it reminds pastors of the need to be quiet and to listen to the other person. We are all to eager to give others the benefit of our wisdom and experience. Even if the advice is good, it is often best given after an attempt has been made to establish a relationship and to understand the other person. It is only then that it may become acceptable. Counselling cannot just be learned from books, and it should be recognized that counselling training and supervision should be available to all who are engaged in pastoral care.

Critics sometimes object that non-directive counselling is inappropriate in Christian pastoral care, for directions have to be given and judgements made. If this were ever true it is no longer so, for, as I have pointed out, modern counsellors, working with 'eclectic models', move on from non-direction to clarifying and directive phases. This is a good model for the pastor, who will often want to move on to give spiritual direction or other forms of advice to those who come to him.

Another objection is that some priests allow counselling to dominate their pastoral work. There is a place for Christian pastors who specialize in this work, and it is good to have such specialists to whom others can refer. Further, there are some settings (some chaplaincies, for example), where it might well be a central task. In relation to the local church setting, the following points need to be made.

Counselling should be seen in the context of the whole work of pastoral ministry: it is distinguished from secular counselling in that it is rooted in the ministries of word and sacraments. The Christian pastor is not a freelance: he operates as the agent of a worshipping community. This does not mean that he has to impose 'religious' solutions upon those he counsels, but honesty and clarity demand that it should be clear on what terms he operates.

Pastoral counselling, in Britain at least, is not usually an affair of appointments and offices, for such help is customarily given in a variety of settings: by a hospital bedside, in a distressed woman's kitchen, as well as in the vicarage study. Not to be tied to an office or an appointments system, and to have access to most people's homes, are great advantages to the parish priest, especially when they are helping those passing through some form of crisis.

A criticism sometimes levelled at counselling is that it can be a means of persuading people to accept an intolerable social situation. A young black, for example, should not be counselled simply to come to terms with his permanent unemployment or his experiences of racial injustice. The counsellor should be prepared to become involved in moves to provide employment or overcome racism, and to criticize injustices in society.

Provided that it does not become merely inward-looking and divorced from social reality, counselling has an important contribution to make to pastoral care. Victorian Anglo-Catholic priests were often paternalistic in their attitudes towards parishioners. They were gentlemen who were sure they knew what was best for their social inferiors. Today priests operate in a less authoritarian and more egalitarian society. The non-authoritarian stance of modern counselling is more appropriate to contemporary social relations. In so far as the priest has occasion to direct others or to teach them, he earns his right to do so from the respect derived from his evident experience and expertise, rather than from traditional notions of authority or social superiority.

FURTHER READING

Michael Jacobs, *Still Small Voice:An Introduction to Pastoral Counselling*, SPCK, 1982

Eugene Kennedy, *Crisis Counselling:An Essential Guide for Non-Professional Counsellors*, Gill and Macmillan, 1981

Kenneth Leech, *Soul Friend:A Study of Spirituality*, Sheldon Press, 1977

Carole Sutton, *Psychology for Social Workers and Counsellors*, Routledge and Kegan Paul, 1981

The book by Michael Jacobs is the first volume of an important new series on pastoral counselling. Ken Leech discusses counselling in relation to spiritual direction. Carole Sutton summarizes recent developments in the psychology of counselling.

10   The Ministry of Reconciliation

From Canon B29 Of the Ministry of Absolution

1. It is the duty of baptised persons at all time to the best of their understanding to examine their lives and conversations by the rule of God's commandments, and whereinsoever they perceive themselves to have offended by will, act, or omission, there to bewail their own sinfulness and to confess themselves to Almighty God with full purpose of amendment of life, that they may receive of him the forgiveness of their sins which he has promised to all who turn to him with hearty repentance and true faith: acknowledging their sins and seeking forgiveness, especially in the general Confessions of the congregation and in the Absolution pronounced by the priest in the services of the Church.

2. If there be any who by these means cannot quiet his own conscience, but requires further comfort or counsel, let him come to some discreet and learned minister of God's Word; that by the ministry of God's holy Word he may receive the benefit of absolution, together with ghostly counsel and advice, to the quieting of his conscience and avoiding of all scruple and doubtfulness.

3. In particular a sick person, if he feels his conscience troubled in any weighty matter, should make a special confession of his sins, that the priest may absolve him if he humbly and heartily desire it.

The Canons of the Church of England

ANGLO-CATHOLICISM AND CONFESSION

Probably the most controversial aspect of the nineteenth-century Anglo-Catholic revival was its reintroduction of the practice of sacramental confession into the Church of England. Both John Keble and Edward Pusey put a great emphasis upon its value in helping the Christian to grow in holiness of life. In doing so they immediately ran into Protestant fears of popery and priestly domination, but they were at pains to point out that what they advocated was fully sanctioned by Anglican authority.

The origins of sacramental confession can be traced to the public penances of the early Church, in which those who had committed grave sins such as apostasy or murder were excluded from the sacraments and made to endure a prolonged period of public penance. This practice evolved into the system of private confession from the fourth century onwards, when the practice developed of confessing all sins, minor as well as major, to a priest who would then assign an appropriate penance and give spiritual advice. By the twelfth century something like the modern practice had developed; the priest gave absolution before a token penance, and absolution was in the indicative form in which the priest forgave the penitent as the agent of God (not merely declaring God's forgiveness, as was the earlier practice).

Anglo-Catholics held that the Reformation Church of England had accepted this practice. The only substantial disagreement with the medieval Church was over making confession compulsory. While emphasizing the spiritual value of sacramental confession, Anglo-Catholics upheld the scriptural teaching that true contrition was in itself sufficient for the reconciliation of sinners with God, and that therefore forgiveness was available apart from sacramental confession.

The Book of Common Prayer was the main authority for commending sacramental confession. In the ordination service 'The Ordering of Priests', three priestly functions were specified: preaching the word, administration of the sacraments (Baptism and the Eucharist), and the discipline of Christ. Discipline, with its reference to Christ's words, 'Whose sin thou dost forgive, they are forgiven; and whose sins thou dost retain they are retained,' was taken to include sacramental confession. The first exhortation of the Holy Communion service concluded with the offer to the congregation that 'if there be any of you, who cannot quiet his own conscience, let him come to me, or to some other discreet and learned Minister of God's Word, and open his grief; that by the ministry of God's holy Word he may receive the benefit of absolution, together with ghostly counsel and advice.'

In the Order for the Visitation of the Sick there was a direction that 'Here shall the sick person be moved to make a special confession of his sins, if he feel his conscience troubled with any weighty matter. After which confession, the priest shall absolve him (if he humbly and heartily desire it).' The form of absolution then given was that normally used by Anglican priests for all confessions: 'Our Lord Jesus Christ, who hath left power to His Church to absolve all sinners who truly repent and believe in Him, of His great mercy forgive thee thine offences; And by His authority committed to me, I absolve thee from all thy sins, in the Name of the Father and of the Son, and of the Holy Ghost. Amen.'

The retention of the indicative form here was taken to be conclusive proof of the intention of the Church of England to retain the Catholic doctrine and practice of sacramental confession. The evidence of the Prayer Book was reinforced by reference to great Anglican teachers such as Hooker and Jeremy Taylor. George Herbert laid it down that 'In his visiting the sick or otherwise afflicted', the Country Parson should follow 'the Church's counsel, namely in persuading them to particular confession, labouring to make them understand the great good use of this ancient and pious ordinance and how necessary it is in some cases.' Despite the efforts of Herbert and other priests of his generation, the practice of confession to a priest had almost completely died out by the end of the seventeenth century, so that when it was revived by the Oxford Movement its use seemed strange and un-Anglican.

From the beginning of his ministry at Wantage W.J. Butler was sure that the revival of confession was of the utmost importance, but he was equally aware of the need for care and tact in introducing it into parochial life. He would wait until he had 'fully gained the love and confidence of his flock'. Although he believed there would be no deepening of the spiritual life of his parish without it, he would not press the idea, nor would he teach that it was absolutely necessary. He would wait patiently for his people to realize their need, for then they would freely avail themselves of the grace and help of the sacrament. He considered there were two sorts of parishioner who particularly needed to quieten their consciences in this way: those who had lived sinful lives and were deeply troubled when their consciences were awakened, and those who were 'very earnestly desiring to lead a higher Christian life' but who were 'vexed by even little faults'.

Gradually the practice was accepted by a minority of his congregation, not only by the sick but also by a small number who made their confessions each month. In the 1870s one of Butler's former curates recorded that in his small Somerset village parish there were about 200 confessions made a year. If this represented about 50 individuals it was about one quarter of the Easter communicants. Butler warned against dealing with confessions 'technically or perfunctorily', as he believed Roman Catholic priests did. He also warned against 'the slightest indecorum with women', or 'pressing in detail with sins to do with the seventh commandment'. It was better to risk an imperfect confession than to suggest sin or scrupulosity. Confessions were normally heard in an open church, the priest seated. The penitent knelt beside him and asked for a blessing. After the confession of his sins, advice was given together with a token penance (often prayers to be said). The absolution then pronounced was that given in the visitation service in the Book of Common Prayer.

Sacramental confession was an important part of Anglo-Catholic pastoral care, although only a minority availed themselves of its grace. Anglo-Catholics were confident of their belief in its importance despite widespread opposition because they could cite the authority of the Book of Common Prayer; but they were careful about the way it was introduced into parochial life and they emphasized its voluntary nature. The same circumspection was not always observed by the later generation of priests, the Ritualists, some of whom followed the Roman line that all must make use of the sacrament. Considerable controversy was caused in the late Victorian period, with Protestant attacks being launched against confession in the House of Lords. Fortunately, these controversies are now dead. The Victorian Anglo-Catholics established that confession is a legitimate part of the Anglican pastoral tradition.

THE SACRAMENT OF RECONCILIATION TODAY

Three terms are used for the subject we are discussing. The sacrament of penance is still the official title in the Roman Catholic Church; it was derived from its dominant feature in the early days of the Church: the imposition and working out of a prolonged and heavy penance for a major sin. The commonly used term 'confession' came into use with the next stage of history when the penance was reduced to a purely nominal exercise and the emphasis was put upon the detailed confession of all sins, minor as well as major. The third term, 'reconciliation', is used increasingly nowadays, and highlights what is now seen to be the chief feature of the sacrament. Jesus came with a message of forgiveness and the first Christians believed that through him God was reconciling men to himself. Confession is seen as a way by which reconciliation is effected as sin is confessed and God's forgiveness given. (It is not the only way, for Baptism and the Eucharist also effect reconciliation.)

In recent years there has been a decline in the numbers using the sacrament of penance in the Roman Catholic Church, due largely to a relaxation of rules but also to dissatisfaction with old ways of administering it. Recently new rites of penance have been published, and new thinking about the sacrament has emerged. It is important for Anglicans to be aware of these changes because, although the sacrament is not widely used by Anglicans, a consideration of recent Roman Catholic thinking makes it clear that there is much to be gained from its use.

Significant changes have come about in two main areas: in thinking about the nature of sin, and in thinking about the sacraments generally. Until recently the emphasis was upon the detailed confession of lists of sins. The dominant image was a legal one: the penitent came to the tribunal of penance to spell out his breaches of the divine law. Now the emphasis is not so exclusively upon particular sins as upon the penitent's inner state. Individual wrong acts are symptoms of an inner division. Moral rules continue to be important as guides, but the way anyone treats them is symptomatic of the state of his whole relationship to God and his fellow men. Sin, in the singular, indicates damaged relationships with God and man, and it is this that underlies particular sins or breaches of the moral law.

There is also a shift from the idea of obedience to a set of rules out of fear, to the idea of wanting to do what is right because it is seen to be right in the context of love of God and man. The overcoming of sin is not so much a matter of ticking off particular sins conquered as a process of conversion. If sin is a state of alienation from God through apathy, forgetfulness or wilful disobedience, then what is needed is a whole-hearted turning to God.

Another new insight into the nature of sin in relation to the sacrament of penance is the idea that sin is not merely an individual affair between a person and God, but that it has communal dimensions. Anyone's behaviour has consequences for others; wrong-doing often hurts not only one person but many others. So confession may also involve mutual expressions of penitence among church members in communal acts of penitence; and even individual confessions contain an element of an acknowledgement of sin against the Church as well as against God.

In accordance with these new attitudes, if confession is not merely a case of going through a check list of sins but going deeper to their underlying causes in alienation from God and inner disharmony, there may need to be more time given to a confession, at least on some occasions, than is usually the case at present. If the confession is to be an occasion of growth and learning there must be time for exploration and discussion.

The modern practice of confession is changing not only as a result of new ideas on sin but also in relation to new thought about the sacraments. In the past it was Roman Catholic teaching that Jesus had instituted each of the seven sacraments as means of grace. Now, alongside traditional doctrine, a new approach has developed from a different starting point. The traditional idea of a sacrament is that it is a 'sacred sign which effects what it symbolizes'. In the new approach the Church is taken to be the basic sacrament, the sacred sign of Christ. It effectively makes Christ present because he works in and through it. The seven sacraments express the basic sacramental nature of the Church because Christ works in and through them in relation to the main events and deepest needs in human life. Men need to confess their sins and receive forgiveness at critical moments in their lives, and also as part of a continuing quest to deepen faith and commitment.

There is also a new view of the way in which sacraments work and become effective in men's lives. The traditional view emphasized the objectivity of the sacramental gift. If a sacrament was valid in terms of having the right minister, matter, form and intention, then grace was guaranteed. All that mattered in confession was that the confessor was a properly authorised priest. It did not matter what he said beyond the correct form of words, nor what the penitent felt beyond the correct intention.

Grace was thought of in impersonal and quantitative terms; so it made sense to go to confession frequently.

Today, without rejecting the truth of the objective nature of the sacrament, the Church pays more attention to the subjective factors involved in order to make the sacrament more effective in men's lives. It is to be an encounter with meaning, not a perfunctory duty. The penitent comes not just to read a list of sins but rather to acknowledge his need for forgiveness and help. This calls for deep sympathy and respect on the part of the confessor, who will try to convey his understanding and acceptance of the penitent. He will try to grant forgiveness not merely by the external gift of absolution, but also by his attitude, helping the penitent to feel forgiven and to be able to forgive himself because he has been forgiven by God and the Church, through the person of the priest.

In the new Roman Catholic rites of penance there is a real attempt to make it possible to establish a more human relationship between priest and penitent. The confessor is called upon to welcome the penitent with kindness and to help him to make his confession. He is to try to give the penitent the chance to voice his problems and requests for help, and to give more time for appropriate counsel and guidance if asked for.

CONFESSION AND PSYCHOTHERAPY

I will conclude this chapter on the sacrament of reconciliation by discussing some questions about the relationship between confession, psychotherapy and counselling. There are many schools of psychotherapy as there are of counselling, but here I shall raise only a few major points which are appropriate to all of them. The broad distinction between psychotherapy and counselling, is that in the former attempts are made to deal with non-conscious thoughts and feelings, whereas counsellors generally restrict themselves to conscious thoughts and motivations.

There are close similarities between the sacrament of reconciliation on the one hand, and psychotherapy and counselling on the other. There is the same basis in a relationship between two persons: priest and penitent, psychotherapist and patient. Both involve self-disclosure and both are meant to lead to some change in the life of the person being helped. It is also true of the sacrament of reconciliation, as of psychotherapy, that change is seen as therapeutic. But there are differences.

The focus in confession is on deliberate wrong-doing, whereas moral judgements are not made in psychotherapy; its focus is on inner conflicts and feelings. Confession is relatively structured and short. The penitent is received, confesses, is given brief counsel, and absolved. A psychotherapeutic session is long and unstructured and is focused upon the patient's free expression of his thoughts and feelings, together with the therapist's reflections and interpretations.

With the attempt to make confession more of a therapeutic relationship, its likeness to psychotherapy will increase. Nevertheless, they are two separate and distinct activities, each with its own purpose and validity. A confessor, like a pastoral counsellor, does not attempt to give the psychotherapy for which he is not usually trained, and makes a point of referring people who are seen to be in need of more expert treatment.

An area of apparent overlap, potential conflict, and misunderstanding centres on the question of guilt. In pastoral care the term usually refers to 'healthy' guilt. It is normal to experience feelings of guilt about things we have done wrong. It is the person who experiences no such feelings, when he has harmed others, who is abnormal. A mature moral person has developed the capacity to feel concern for others; his conscience causes him to feel guilt and shame concerning the actual harm done to them. In the confessional, in prayers of confession, in informal discussion with a pastor, our normal guilt feelings help us to recognize and feel sorry for wrong done to others and to God.

The psychotherapist is more likely to be dealing with distorted 'pathological' feelings of guilt. His depressed patients experience anxiety and feelings of guilt, not in relation to acual acts of wrong-doing, but generally and all-pervasively. It is this free-floating miasma of guilt feelings which the psychotherapist seeks to dissipate.

Some forms of religion have in fact produced pathological guilt. Authoritarian religious ideas, which picture God as an unbending tyrant or judge and which coerce people through the fear of hell, are likely to produce pathological forms of guilt. Much Victorian religion was of this type. God was held to be paticularly angry about 'the sins of the flesh'. Some Evangelicals pressed for conversions, and some Anglo-Catholics pressed people into making their confession, by inducing fear and irrational feelings of guilt. This kind of religion is liable to foster depression and neurosis.

This is a large question and I have only touched on it superficially, but the main point is clear: there need be no conflict between pastoral care and psychotherapy on the question of guilt, once it is understood what each side means by the term.

Confessors are sometimes referred to as physicians of souls. The findings about the qualities needed to be an effective counsellor (non-possessive warmth; genuine concern and empathy) help us to see how the sacrament of reconciliation can be made a more effective therapeutic encounter. For these findings show that, given the right attitudes on the part of the pastor, the penitent may be enabled to grow as a person. We are alerted to the importance of the quality of the relationship. A distant, or aloof, or merely 'professional' confessor is likely to inhibit rather than help the growth of the penitent.

Unconditional acceptance means that a deep respect is shown for the person who has come to confess. He is accepted as a person even though the fact that he has done wrong is acknowledged. Often penitents find it hard to accept and forgive themselves; religious people sometimes hate themselves. Acceptance and non-possessive warmth on the part of the confessor create an atmosphere in which a penitent may begin to be able to accept and forgive himself. Anglo-Catholics in the nineteenth century, by overreacting against Evangelicalism, did not fully appreciate the truth in the idea of justification by faith: that we are acceptable because God accepts us whatever or whoever we are. The counsellor's accepting attitude mediates God's acceptance.

Genuine concern means that the priest shows himself transparently as a follower of Christ. He does not hide behind a facade of clerical 'professionalism'. He is mature enough to recognize his own fallibility: this makes him approachable. Empathy refers to the priest's ability to put himself imaginatively in the penitent's place: to see the other's problems from the other's perspective.

In the sacrament of reconciliation, as in other pastoral relationships, the pastor is more than a functionary administering a rite or dispensing a service. His human attitudes are important in helping people to gain the confidence to turn fear and self-preoccupation into faith and confidence and love.

FURTHER READING

D. Constant and D. Dodgson, *Forgiveness:The Sacrament of Penance Today*, Mayhew-McCrimmon, 1976

M. Hebblethwaite and K. Donovan, *The Theology of Penance*, Mercier Press, 1979

K. Leech, *Soul Friend:A Study of Sprituality*, Sheldon Press, 1977

The first two books provide good short accounts of recent Roman Catholic developments. Ken Leech adds an Anglican commentary.

11 The Care of the Dying and Bereaved

Canon B37 Of the Ministry to the Sick

1. The minister shall use his best endeavours to ensure that he be speedily informed when any person is sick or in danger of death in the parish, and shall as soon as possible resort unto him to exhort, instruct, and comfort him in his distress in such manner as he shall think most needful and convenient.

2. When any person sick or in danger of death or so impotent that he cannot go to church is desirous of receiving the most comfortable sacrament of the Body and Blood of Christ, the priest, having knowledge therof, shall as soon as may be visit him, and unless there be any grave reason to the contrary, shall reverently minister the same to the said person at such place and time as may be convenient.

3. If any such person so desires, the priest may lay hands upon him and may anoint him with oil on the forehead with the sign of the Cross using a form of service authorised by Canon B1 and using pure olive oil consecrated by the bishop of the diocese or otherwise by the priest himself in accordance with such form of service.

The Canons of the Church of England

THE PASTORAL CARE OF THE DYING

At Easter in 1852 Karl Marx's little daughter Franziska died in the family rooms in Dean Street, Soho. His wife Jenny recorded in her diary that 'Her small lifeless body

78

rested in our little back room, whilst we all went together into the front room, and when night came, we made up our beds on the floor. The three surviving children lay with us, and we cried for the poor little angel who now rested, cold and lifeless, in the next room.' In 1852 there was nothing unusual in such an experience, especially for the poor. High mortality rates, lack of hospital facilities and crowded conditions acquainted almost everyone with the reality of death.

Since then there has been a dramatic change. Mortality rates among the young have been vastly reduced, about half of all deaths take place in hospital, and those who die at home sometimes do so in isolation. Death is no longer an everyday reality and it has become a subject we are reluctant to discuss or think about, for it does not fit into our image of life as we would like it to be.

A famous legend about Gautama the Buddha tells how his father sought to shield him from all the unpleasant realities of life by enclosing him in a garden of pleasures. However, Gautama persuaded his chariot driver to take him into the outside world, where he saw four sights which led him to break with his old life and to seek enlightenment: a sick man, an old man, a corpse, and a holy man. From these he learned that life was transient, inevitably ending in sickness, old age and death. The worldly life was an illusion, and the spiritual life alone led to happiness.

We in the secularized West have to make an effort of imagination to understand Buddhist teaching on death. In the same way we find it difficult to understand the Christian tradition and the importance it assigned to death in pastoral care. For us death is a defeat: we have almost come to accept the illusion that medical science can ward it off for ever. In what follows I shall explain what was believed and done in the past about the pastoral care of the dying, and then consider the relevance of this tradition today.

The visitation of the sick and dying has always been a serious obligation for parish priests. The Book of Common Prayer and the 1601 canons of the Church of England laid it down that the priest was to be informed when anyone was sick, and that he must visit them in order 'to instruct and comfort them in their distress'. In 1661 Bishop Jeremy Taylor advised that the pastor 'ought to be careful in visiting all the sick and afflicted persons of his parish', and he 'must not stay till he be sent for, but of his own accord, go to them'. In 1692 Bishop Gilbert Burnet made it clear that 'One of the chief parts of the Pastoral Care, is the visiting of the sick.'

The reason why this was so important was that it was believed that after death there would be a judgement, at which souls would be assigned either to heaven or hell. Life on earth was a time of probation leading to its crucial closing moments. The pastoral task was to ensure that the faithful did not despair nor lapse from faith, and that the wicked and lukewarm were brought to faith and repentance.

The priest's task was outlined in 'The Order for the Visitation of the Sick' in the Book of Common Prayer. He was to remind the sick person that his illness was a visitation from God to lead him to repentance, and that he ought to endure with patience. He was to be moved to confess his sins, to be given absolution and prepared to receive Holy Communion.

Anglo-Catholics like W.J. Butler took this ministry very seriously indeed. 'Godly persons' were gently reminded of the purpose of 'God's visitation' and having been given absolution they received Holy Communion. In 1865 Butler recounted how an 'intelligent and humble Christian' died 'ready for the call'. Having 'received the Blessed Sacrament' he 'passed away in rest and peace'.

R.W. Randall, the first vicar of the famous Anglo-Catholic church of All Saints, Clifton, recorded his ten visits to a mortally ill young woman. He began by telling her that her illness was sent by God to lead her to repentance. Over the following three visits he instructed her until she was ready to confess 'with signs of contrition'. Several sessions were then spent on preparation for Holy Communion, which she received with joy. Her final days were spent in penitence, thankfulness and 'in the peace of the Lord'.

Priests wrestled with those who had led sinful lives, and sometimes succeeded in bringing them to repentance. In 1848 W.J. Butler recorded how a delirious and dying drunk had been brought into the workhouse. When he was abandoned by the doctor, Butler prayed that he would be spared long enough to repent. Gradually, the man was able to talk about his past life, and he confessed his sins. Although a mass of putrefying sores, he accepted his sufferings with patience and humility.

Often the most difficult cases were those who saw no need to repent and who thought 'they would go to rest' automatically. Butler, and other priests, blamed this attitude on ignorance and the disastrous evangelical doctrine of assurance, which led people to rely on feelings rather than acts of will in repentance.

I have described this phase of traditional pastoral care in some detail because throughout Christian history pastors have paid great attention to it. Today it is an aspect of the ministry we approach with some uncertainty.

The modern Christian pastor has the very responsible task of caring for the dying in a situation where many of them have little or no idea of Christian teaching about death and its significance. At one time pastors could take a belief in life after death for granted; today many people have no belief or one that is extremely tenuous. The pastor's task is not to force this belief upon the reluctant, but to have thought it through carefully for himself, so that he can discuss the Christian view with conviction. In recent years Christian philosophers and theologians, like John Hick and H.D. Lewis, have presented carefully reasoned defences of traditional ideas about the after-life.

If there is a God who is a God of love, it seems reasonable to believe that he will not allow death to terminate the relationship we have begun to establish with him. An important way to reassure the dying is to help them to develop and consolidate their relationship with God. Many dying people wish for prayers to be said for them and with

81

them. They appreciate readings from scripture, help to confess sins and to effect reconciliations, and the administration of Holy Communion.

Although the pastor's primary resource is his knowledge of God gained through the reading of scripture, the practice of prayer and worship, and the study of theology, he also needs to be aware of psychological and other studies of the process of dying. These help in understanding various reactions to the realization that one is dying, ranging from evasion through rejection to acceptance.

Dying can be a time of growth in which old hatreds and resentments melt away and some kind of life-affirmation is achieved. A sensitive pastor can help a person to achieve reconciliation to himself, to others and to God. Nevertheless, there are limits to what can be achieved, for the way people die is usually of a piece with the way they lived. What is of paramount importance is that the freedom and dignity of the dying person should be respected.

THE PASTORAL CARE OF THE BEREAVED

Although the care of the sick and dying figured prominently in traditional accounts of pastoral care, not much was written about work with the bereaved.

In the past the focal point of pastoral care with the bereaved was the burial service itself. Its words and actions affirmed Christian beliefs about life after death, and enabled mourners to say a final farewell to the departed in commending them to God. The service was followed by recognized mourning customs which allowed time for grieving and readjustment, before reintegration into the community.

These beliefs and customs were taken for granted: there was no need to discuss them. Today there is more discussion, partly because psychological and sociological studies have equipped us with more knowledge about bereavement, and partly because traditional beliefs and customs are no longer taken for granted. Many old mourning customs have fallen into disuse in our less formal society. This modern informality deprives mourners of the assistance of generally recognized patterns of behaviour. Well-meaning neighbours who wish to help them find themselves at a loss.

Helping the bereaved is an extremely important aspect of pastoral care, which needs careful attention on the part of the parish priest and all concerned with this work in the parish.

After the death, contact should be established with the family as soon as possible to offer whatever counsel is needed. The details of the service should be discussed carefully so that the family can take part with greater understanding. Of course this is often not possible in large parishes with non-churchgoing families, but it does represent the initial care that can be offered where it is possible and practicable.

The funeral service is not primarily an occasion to eulogize the departed but, in the context of an act of worship, to give thanks for his life and to commend him into the care of God. The words of the service and its reverent conduct comfort by conveying the assurance that there is a meaning and purpose even in death. The rite marks a definite point where the bereaved can begin the process of letting-go the departed.

After the burial the bereaved are often numbed. Gradually in the course of the subsequent weeks those most closely concerned (widows and widowers, for example) awake to a full realization of what has happened. Here psychological studies of the process of mourning can be of great help in assisting the Christian community in the practice of effective and responsible pastoral care.

The bereaved need to work through their feelings about the departed: they should be encouraged to express their feelings of desolation, of guilt and resentment. It is no help to distract them with chat or with easy consolation. It is natural to grieve and grief should not be interpreted as a failure of Christian hope. The biblical view of death is that it is unnatural and contrary to God's intention. It is to be treated seriously, for man is not

83

a soul imprisoned in a body for whom immortality is automatic, but someone who really dies and who awaits resurrection. We wait in hope, but the darkness of grief has to be faced.

CONCLUSION

The care of the dying was one of the most important parts of traditional pastoral care. Under the influence of the Oxford Movement, parish priests made a strong point of carrying through all the rites prescribed in the Book of Common Prayer in relation to the sick and dying. Similarly, the care of the bereaved was centred on the rites of the burial service. These rituals (or modern versions of them) remain central to the cure of souls.

Nowadays there are other considerations to be borne in mind. Parish priests need to have a carefully considered understanding of the Christian faith in order to help the dying and the bereaved. In a post-Christian society there is an even greater need than before to help parishioners to attain a personal and mature faith. Pastoral workers can be aided in their work by a knowledge and understanding of modern methods of counselling and studies of dying and bereavement.

One important topic I have not touched upon in this chapter, and can do no more than mention here, is the modern revival of the anointing of the sick. One of the longer-term benefits of the Oxford Movement was the stimulus it gave to the revival of this ancient rite. The Reformers rejected it because it had become simply the anointing of the dying. In this century the Anglican Church has recovered this rite as part of its ministry to all the sick (and not just to the dying).

FURTHER READING

I. Ainsworth-Smith and P. Speck, *Letting Go:Caring for the Dying and Bereaved*, SPCK, 1982

N. Autton, *A Handbook of Sick Visiting*, Mowbray, 1981

John Hick, *Death and Eternal Life*, Collins, 1976

12 Charity, Social Work and Social Justice

CHARITY

The care of the poor was central to the teachings of the Old Testament prophets and of Jesus himself. In the early Church collections were taken for the poor at the Eucharist and distributed by deacons on behalf of their bishops. The Church had numerous needy members, for persecutions left many Christians destitute as a result of the confiscation of goods or the death of husbands or parents.

In the Middle Ages the bishops' responsibilities expanded as the Church grew in power and numbers: the early Church was responsible only for its own members, but now all members of society were reckoned to be members of the Church. Some bishops made considerable efforts to help by establishing travellers' hostels, orphanages and hospitals. Parish priests gave away money and looked after the sick. Until the thirteenth century the Church had sole responsiblity for the care of the poor but, towards the end of the Middle Ages, the problems of poverty associated with the growth of towns became so great that town authorities and prosperous laymen had to step in to assist with charitable relief and with the running of hospitals. The clergy were still closely involved and the combined efforts of Church and civil authorities meant that the poor were often very well provided for in relation to the standards of the time.

After the Reformation it was at first decreed that parish officials should assist the poor out of funds collected by the clergy as alms, but under Queen Elizabeth I the civil authorities took full control under the new Poor Law.

Nevertheless in the seventeeth century the clergy still had important responsibilities, for the government left the implementation of the Poor Law to local officers, church-wardens and overseers, with the clergy as their agents. George Herbert wrote that the country parson was to be 'full of charity'. On rising in the morning, he was to think about what good deeds he could do that day.

He first considers his own parish, and takes care that all be in a competent way of getting their living. This he effects either by bounty or persuasion, or by authority, making use of that excellent statute which binds all parishes to maintain their own. As well as this general provision, he hath other times of opening his hand, as at great festivals and Com-munions . . . at hard times and deaths he even parts his living and life amongst them, giving some corn outright, and selling other at under rates; and when his own stock serves not, working those that are able to the same charity, still pressing it in the pulpit and out of the pulpit, and never leaving them till he obtained his desire.

In the eighteenth and nineteenth centuries the problem of poverty took on a new dimension with the growth of industrialization. Previously the poor were largely those like the aged and orphans, who could not work. Now there were increasing numbers of able-bodied unemployed swelling the ranks of paupers. The provisions of the Poor Law were harsh and inadequate and were supple-mented by an enormous amount of charitable work, usually inspired and provided by Christians. In 1865 the Charity Organization Society was formed to try to regulate some of this activity. The leaders of this group argued that charitable giving was often haphazard and indiscriminate. Much that was channelled through the churches was seen by the poor as a bribe to get them to attend church services. The Charity Organization Society developed a method of interview, the forerunner of modern social casework, in which each case was carefully assessed on its merits. If the person concerned was deemed to be deserving of relief, then he was directed to the appropriate relief agency.

The cause of poverty was believed to be moral failure: if a man was poor it was because of some personal fault, such as drunkenness, improvidence, or laziness, which had to be eradicated before his position could be improved. Indiscriminate giving merely encouraged immorality. Only the deserving poor were to be helped: that is, those who could show that they were poor through no fault of their own. It was believed that the sole long-term cure for most poverty was the moral reclamation of the poor.

There is something of this distinction between the deserving and the undeserving poor in Herbert's *Country Parson*. At one point he argued that 'in all his charity' the parson should favour those 'who live best, and take most pains'. But for the most part the emphasis in Herbert's work was chiefly the traditional Catholic one, that it was the Christian's duty to be liberal and charitable, 'for we are more enjoined to be charitable than wise'. This tradition influenced later priests like the late-Victorian Anglo-Catholic, Charles Marson, who fiercely denounced the whole approach of the Charity Organization Society. However, most parish priests agreed with its diagnosis of the cause of poverty, and encouraged the poor to be thrifty by setting up clothing, food and coal clubs, and other forms of self-help.

From the beginning of the twentieth century both the traditional Christian approach to poverty and Victorian moralism were forced to give way to new attitudes and systems of provision. Social surveys, undertaken at the turn of the century, showed that the cause of mass poverty had more to do with problems associated with the structure of society than with the failings of individuals. About 30 per cent of the population in London and York had a standard of living below that of mere subsistence, due to low wages and involuntary unemployment. Such a vast problem obviously could not be solved by charitable effort and moral reformation alone. The solution was a change in the structure of society to ensure a fairer distribution of incomes and support from the state. What later came to be called the Welfare State was set up to deal with these problems; along with it a network of social services was established, together with a new profession of social worker. In the course of the century the parish clergy have lost much of their importance in charitable activity, and recently the role of the churches in social work has been further eroded. What is the place of this aspect of the Christian tradition of pastoral care today?

SOCIAL WORK

The practical expression of Christian love through social work is an indispensable feature of pastoral ministry. Karl Rahner has argued that 'it remains true to say that a pastoral activity that is purely religious in character and expressed in preaching and the sacramental ministry alone is in a certain sense too abstract' (*Theological Investigations*, Vol. 10, 1973, p. 362.) If this is the case, how is the Church to exercise this aspect of its pastoral responsiblity now that the state and secular agencies have largely taken over? Before dealing with this question it is necessary to clarify what should be the Church's attitude towards the secular social services.

We have seen how Victorian Anglo-Catholics fought a rearguard action against the loss of their monopoly in education; some showed a similar proprietary attitude towards the administration of charity. Their medieval views bore little relation to reality, for the state alone commanded the necessary resources to meet the needs of an expanding and complex society. Since the Second World War the Welfare State has aimed at comprehensive provision for its citizens 'from the cradle to the grave'. Yet these developments should not be seen negatively as loss by the Church. The assumption that the Church has to be in control implies that God works only though ecclesiastical institutions: secularization, the loss of control by the Church over sectors of society, then means the exit of God from the world. Karl Rahner suggested that 'The Church can freely . . . leave to the world in its growing worldliness much social work which at one time she did perform, for in fact she herself wills the world to develop along these lines. She does not need to be anxious . . . lest she should be surrendering something which she is bound to perform for all time' (p. 362).

The secular world must be allowed to stand on its own feet. The Church provided social services when the state was too undeveloped to do so, but now the state is capable of taking over for itself. God's grace is not shut up in ecclesiastical institutions: we 'should not suppose that the realities signified by the terms "Christian" and "ecclesiastical" are co-extensive'. An unrecognized grace can be embodied in the secular social services. For even when God's presence is not explicitly recognized it is still possible to affirm he is at work.

> For everywhere where secular social activities of the community contribute to the abiding dignity of the person, his freedom and his liberation from a state of alienation from himself, where they enable man to be himself and to pursue his earthly and eternal lot in self-responsibility, where they free him as much as possible of the burden of the pre-personal element in order to lay upon him the heaviest burden of them all, himself in his own freedom — in all these areas factors are objectively present in the life of society which are also capable of embodying love, and often actually do so. And in doing so they are capable of belonging to the form in which the Church manifests herself, even though this significance in them is quite unrecognised (p. 362).

God is to be seen in all social work inspired by self-giving love. Through the well-established methods of social casework (similar to counselling), and the more recent practices of group work and community work, social workers set out to 'contribute to the abiding dignity of the person' by bringing about 'his freedom and his liberation' and so enabling him to 'be himself'. Their aim is to increase their client's 'self-responsibility' so that he can act freely and in a fully personal way. Social work is not about doing things for others or making gifts in a way that will make them dependent but about increasing the area of freedom and responsibility by helping people to decide and act for themselves. To do this for another human being is to be moved by God's grace, for God is at work in all who are open to him. The Church has a special role as the sacramental sign of God, but it does not mark the boundary of his operations.

The Church does not, therefore, have to set up rival social services alongside those of the state, for it can recognize that God's work is done through secular agencies. This recognition should lead the local church to show a special concern for social workers in its area, by getting to know them and providing facilities for discussion of ethical and theological topics relevant to social work. Many social workers have taken up their vocation as an expression of Christian faith and it is incumbent upon the Church to support them in all ways possible.

The clergy should refer cases of need to local social workers and in turn offer help from the church community. As social service budgets contract, the need for voluntary help increases. In many areas local churches co-operate effectively with the statutory services. A community development project was set up for the whole city of Nottingham, working through local caring groups. It was most successful in an old-established working-class area of the town, where a voluntary service scheme was based upon existing church groups and networks of neighbours. In co-operation with the local social services department, they ran lunch and social clubs and a day centre for old people, as well as visiting them in their homes. In Rochester a voluntary 'Hands' scheme was set up through the co-operation of the social services department, the local churches and others, in which a team of befrienders was built up as a means of mutual help in the neighbourhood.

While the Church should not attempt to rival the statutory social services (even if it could), there is still room for some Church-based full-time social work provided on a diocesan or deanery basis. Traditionally diocesan social workers cared for unmarried mothers and arranged adoptions. With the changes in attitudes to unmarried mothers, the increase in abortions, together with loss of functions to statutory social service departments, this work has declined, but new areas of work open up with changing social needs and problems. There is a good case for the Church to retain a stake in social work, particularly in a pioneering capacity, as a concrete expression of its pastoral ministry and as a way of maintaining a link with the social services. Social work is a practical activity, drawing upon a range of social sciences — sociology, social administration, psychology — for its theoretical base. These disciplines are autonomous and independent of theology or Christian faith; nevertheless, social work makes assumptions about the nature of man which are illuminated by theology and Christian ethics. There is a need for social workers and priests capable of informed involvement in these issues; of giving guidance to the local churches; and of pioneering new forms of social work.

SOCIAL JUSTICE

In the earlier discussion of counselling I argued that counselling can be manipulation: helping someone to adjust to, and accept, a situation which should really be changed. Similar criticisms are made of social work. At the turn of the century, there were three attitudes to the treatment of poverty: the traditional approach of handing out relief; the casework approach of the Charity Organization Society; and the new ideas of positive state intervention to provide for the exigencies of life, such as unemployment, widowhood and old age. The first approach, based on old ideas of charity, gave way to the third, based on the idea of justice. In the Victorian period independent spirits among the poor rejected handouts from the rich and demanded 'justice not charity'. The Church needed the stimulus of socialism to recall her to her own tradition of social thought. In 1891 Pope Leo XIII published the first of a series of papal social encyclicals in which the application of the principles of social justice were spelt out. In a just society goods should be so distributed that no-one was forced to live at a level below that of bare subsistence. Wages should not be pushed as low as employers could force them, but should reach a minimum level such that a worker could provide for the basic needs of himself and his family and have a little more to obtain property of his own.

The problem of poverty acquired a new dimension with the advent of industrial societies: old problems worsened and new ones were created. Traditional systems of charitable relief were wholly inadequate, but industrialization provided the means of solving the problem. It is now possible, as never before, for the state to guarantee basic social security.

Christians cannot look for detailed guidance on these questions to the New Testament, for the biblical world was quite different from ours, with neither the same scale of problems nor the same means of solving them. Jesus, as the Old Testament prophets had been before him, was concerned for the poor and warned against riches, but being a man of his time he did not consider the wider problems of social justice. Nevertheless, the principles of social justice, expressed in modern Christian thought, are a legitimate application of Jesus' teaching for our own time. In modern developed societies charitable relief should not be necessary: social justice demands a basic minimum of provision for all, as of right. However, social work will not disappear, for even radical social change will not solve all problems. There will always be those who for one reason or another are unable to cope, and for whom the services of social workers will be required. Nevertheless, radical criticism pinpoints the need to look beyond the problems of the individual in order to make a critical appraisal of the wider social context in which he lives.

Let me try to summarize some of the main findings and implications of this chapter. Christians have always had a concern for the poor and needy. In modern society charitable relief has been replaced by basic social security and social work. The role of the local church is to support and co-operate with statutory and voluntary social services, seeing in them the work of God in the world. This is an area in which the churches in a deanery, together with the churches of other denominations, should co-operate. Representatives of local churches should meet together regularly to identify local needs and co-ordinate their efforts to meet them.

The Church has always recognized its wider duty towards society. Victorians, like Butler, took the traditional view that the Church should support the existing social order. Now, as the Church disengages itself from identification with those in power, it is in a better position to take a more independent stance. Local churches ought to provide a forum for continuous and informed discussion of social issues. If they are involved in the life of their districts they will discover problems which require alleviation, not merely in terms of social work, but also through constructive criticism and social action. There is an immense amount of poverty and injustice in our society and throughout the world, but most church members are hardly aware of it. One of the most important legacies of the Oxford Movement was the concern for social justice that it inspired in the Anglo-Catholic social theology of men like Bishop Gore, Stewart Headlam and Conrad Noel. While the early Anglo-Catholics remained wedded to a conservative medieval ideal, later thinkers drew out the radical social implications of Catholic incarnational and sacramental theology. There has been something of a revival and development of this tradition in recent years, but an immense amount of work remains to be done in terms of introducing a serious social concern into the life of local churches. This is an area which calls out for ecumenical and inter-parish co-operation.

FURTHER READING

Jean S. Heywood, *Casework and Pastoral Care*, SPCK, 1967

Kenneth Leech, *The Social God*, Sheldon Press, 1981

Michael Paget-Wilkes, *Poverty, Revolution and the Church*, Paternoster Press, 1981

Karl Rahner, *Theological Investigations*, vol. X (chapter 18) Darton, Longman and Todd, 1973

Jean Heywood deals with the relationship between secular social work and the Church's pastoral care. Ken Leech provides a modern re-statement of the Anglo-Catholic tradition of social theology. Michael Paget-Wilkes is an Evangelical parish priest who has worked out a social theology in the context of an inner-city parish.

13 Pastoral Care and the Parish Then and Now

In the late 1840s many young Anglican priests, like Jacob Clements of Upton St Leonards and William John Butler of Wantage, entered the pastoral ministry fired by the ideals of the Oxford Movement. Their aim was to reclaim England for the Catholic Church in the parish. They set out to realize George Herbert's vision of the parish church as the soul of the local community, with all aspects of life ordered under the parson's paternal authority.

However, this vision belonged to a passing order of society. Even as Clements and Butler built their schools and administered their charities, England was changing into a modern, industrial urban and secular society.

The next generation of Anglo-Catholic priests were much more aware of these changes. In 1885 the Vicar of Leeds, John Gott, delivered a famous series of lectures on the problems and opportunities of the parish priest of the town. The ills of the parish he diagnosed as the failure to win the working class, the growth of religious doubt and unbelief, and the massive problem of poverty. Nevertheless he was optimistic: dedicated spiritually-minded priests would yet win through.

Twenty years later optimism still prevailed. Cosmo Gordon Lang (later to become Archbishop of Canterbury) wrote of the opportunity of the Church of England. Gott's problems had yet to be overcome, but liberal Anglo-Catholicism, complete with an acceptance of biblical criticism, evolutionary science and the need for social reform, together with efficient parochial machinery, still had a chance of success.

Optimism ended with the First World War. Today no parish church commands the active allegiance of more than a small minority of parishioners. The mass of workers do no more than patronize the rites of passage in decreasing numbers. A small minority of the middle class remain to form the active nucleus of church life. The Church's stake in education and social work and its general social influence are all greatly diminished.

The vision of a restored Christendom in which the parish church nurtured all local inhabitants from the cradle to the grave has faded. It was after all the product of a particular historical situation. In the early Middle Ages Christianity was imposed by rulers upon their subjects and the Church took over the role of the civic religion of the Roman Empire. The social situation which produced Christendom has wholly disappeared. The Oxford Movement shared a common romantic and conservative vision of an idealized rural past in reaction against the supposed evils of the new industrial society.

Anglo-Catholics have now, for the most part, disengaged themselves from that vision. The Church has to work as a small minority, not seeking to turn the clock back but looking forward to the Kingdom of God. In the light of its mission as servant of the Kingdom the Church's role is seen not as the cement of the old order but as an independent agent of God's order.

One aspect of the Anglo-Catholic ideal of Christendom was the belief that non-Anglican religious bodies ought not to exist. Butler worked to make Wantage parish church so strong that the chapels would collapse for lack of support. In the light of an improved theological understanding we now accept our fellow Christians of other denominations, seek to learn from them and work with them as much as we can.

Much of the social vision of the mid-nineteenth century Anglo-Catholics, like their attitude towards other Christians, and also the authoritarian and paternalistic bearing of parish priests, was largely the product of a body of conservative views and attitudes widely accepted at the time but hardly credible today. This is not to conclude, however, that the Oxford Movement has nothing to teach us about pastoral care. The main argument of this book has been that although the pastoral care of the Victorian age was inevitably conditioned by the society in which it was exercized, and has lost some of its relevance, nevertheless its essential insights still have a great deal to say to us.

Anglo-Catholicism recovered the idea of the centrality of sacraments in pastoral care. The ramifications of this insight have still to be fully explored. A growing point in recent thought about pastoral care is a recovered sense of the importance of the corporate and liturgical dimensions of the cure of souls.

The high church insistence on the priority of teaching and the need for it to be given in the context of worship has not diminished in importance. Between us and our early Victorian predecessors lies a history of changes in teaching methods, biblical study and theology. Nevertheless the importance of a life-long education in the Christian tradition has grown in importance in a society where individuals have to be able to stand on their own feet in matters of faith.

It is no less true that the earlier concern to foster personal spiritual development, to care for the individuals's inner life, has not declined in importance. New ideas on psychology, counselling and moral theology have produced changes in approach, but there is a continuity of intent.

My aim in this book has been to recall the pastoral achievements of the Oxford Movement and its followers, and to chart some of the ways in which Catholic pastoral care is being renewed today. It is a story of constant change as society and the church change, and deepest continuity in the essentials.

Index

100